The Amazing Story

of the

Kitchener Poster

The life and times of Britain's most famous image –
Alfred Leete's 'Your Country Needs You'

by

Martyn Thatcher and Anthony Quinn

Funfly Design
www.funfly.co.uk

The Amazing Story of the Kitchener Poster

by

Martyn Thatcher and Anthony Quinn

First published in Great Britain

by Funfly Design,

Chester

2013

ISBN 978-0-9569094-2-8

Contents

Foreword

The original artwork drawn by Alfred Leete in September 1914 (Imperial War Museum)

The name 'Kitchener' and the phrase 'Your Country Needs You' are retained in our collective memory like ghosts. The words are echoes of the First World War and a history that is still within the living memory of a few, but these words come from a world that was a very different place from the one we occupy today. This book will explore that world through a remarkable image – a pencil-and-wash drawing by the cartoonist and commercial artist Alfred Leete that was created for the front cover of *London Opinion*, a weekly humorous magazine. The name, the words and the image have influenced billions of people across the world for a century. They are continually repeated: in a sign seeking staff for a shop on a London high street; on a village notice board in Suffolk seeking volunteers for a village fete; in the advertising for a sitcom based around three recruitment dodgers in World War One.

In writing about this subject, we paint a picture of the lifestyles enjoyed by people at the time. In our exploration we have delved into events that surrounded the British recruitment campaign to offer glimpses of the Edwardian era – when cars and telephones were still rare and magazines and tabloid newspapers were the new media – and so offer a perspective of events from that time.

We have examined many theories about the poster and about the war itself and have tried to go back to the original artefacts – be they the Leete artwork itself, the actual magazines, posters and newspapers, as well as printed and photographic records and commentary.

2

We explore these stories to determine how this picture has become an icon of the First World War. The National Art Library at the Victoria and Albert Museum, the Imperial War Museum, the St Bride Printing Library, British Library Newspapers and the British Library have all been vital to this work. Alongside these resources, the authors' own collections of Kitchener image ephemera and magazines have also contributed.

In a recent book about the subject, James Taylor writes that Leete's Kitchener poster, often credited with being the most popular design of World War I and one that today symbolises the recruitment of millions of men for active service, was, in fact, only produced with a small print run and was rarely seen at the time. The theory is that it became well known only after the Great War, mainly because of publicity by the Imperial War Museum, a suggestion made in 1997 by Nicholas Hiley in the Imperial War Museum Review and repeated by James Aulich and John Hewitt in their 2007 book on Great War posters. It does, however, stretch the imagination to suggest that a poster so well known should not even have existed and that the written and spoken memoirs of war veterans were wrong, due, possibly, to ailing memories. There is good evidence to challenge the theory and we look at this claim in more detail and, hopefully, provide some answers.

This book combines the research of two authors each with expertise in the subject. Of course, the information hasn't suddenly 'popped' into our heads and in addition to our own research we have reviewed and digested the work of others, often contained in articles that did not themselves enjoy a wide circulation, thus this book offers a comprehensive, up to date, and, we believe, an unbiased, account.

In writing the book, the authors have come across several Kitchener posters claiming to be from WWI but which are, in fact, fakes. People producing their own versions tend to use a copy of Leete's artwork downloaded from the Imperial War Museum's website. The artwork has at some stage been damaged and the appearance of these marks gives a way of dating the image. Several organisations and people have kindly given us permission to cite their works and, in addition to offering our thanks here, we give a full list in the Bibliography and Acknowledgements.

However, in interpreting these sources and artefacts, we – and you – cannot undo the influences that have formed our thinking no matter how hard we try, so we leave you to make your own decisions as to what to accept, doubt or seek to challenge.

Martyn Thatcher,

Winsford, Cheshire

Anthony Quinn,

Borough, London

3

Introduction

Figure 1. Alfred Leete's 'Kitchener' cover for London Opinion (1914)

From the thousands of recruiting posters produced in World War One, why has just one become an icon of that conflict? That is the primary question this book sets out to address. This book is about the image on that famous poster, a pencil-and-wash drawing by the magazine cartoonist and commercial artist Alfred Leete that dates back to 1914. The image is of a mustachioed man staring straight at us, his eyes seemingly following us, his finger demanding attention. For Britons and much of the Commonwealth, that man is Lord Kitchener and the artist is Alfred Leete; for people in North America it is Uncle Sam, with a version by James Montgomery Flagg of the thin, white-bearded man that had been a favourite of cartoonists in Europe and the US for decades. Some variant of the words 'Your country needs YOU' may be blazoned across the poster and in our memories. Even outside the English-speaking world, across Europe, Africa and Asia, the formulation is still familiar. This image, and its many variants, with similar words, has been used to sell a multitude of goods and events from local jumble sales to cigarettes to Swinging Sixties clothes to television programmes. It has enjoined people to reject war, as well as fight in more than one, and to reject or accept many theories and ideas. Without doubt, it is a great poster, described by some experts as the best and most effective poster yet seen. This image was created for the September 5 front cover of *London Opinion*, a weekly humorous magazine, soon after war had been declared against Germany in 1914 (Figure 1). Yet, that rushed image of the austere Lord Kitchener and the four words below it – 'Your country needs YOU' – have influenced the minds of billions of people across the world for a century.

Yet, it is a very unusual poster. Almost every advertisement will try to persuade you that you need the product on offer. In the case of Leete's Kitchener poster, the situation is reversed – the man on the poster is claiming to need you! Furthermore, much of the writing about 'the Kitchener poster' and 'Your country needs you' is confused, often conflating different variations of the image and wording, and even totally different posters.

So, many questions arise. What is the power of this image? How did it come about and how did it become such a global icon? Was it widely distributed? Did the real Kitchener actually look like that? This book will explore such questions and also deal with our perceptions of historical events and how, like Chinese whispers, they can change with repetition over time.

How and why has this happened? It is impossible to reach back into the minds of these people and the historical record is patchy. Among the sources there are commercial actors that may have wanted to exaggerate their influence, and individuals who similarly want to expand or minimise their roles or the influence of Leete's work on their own. The government's poster campaign, its advertising propaganda and even the editors and contributors of the popular newspapers and magazines can all claim to have contributed to persuading British men to volunteer for slaughter on the Western Front. This book seeks to go back to the original artefacts – be they the artwork itself, the actual magazines, posters and newspapers, as well as printed and photographic records and commentary – to explore the image and its influence.

Key to this approach is the central chapter based on a timeline. It sets out the main events in a time sequence, which aims to clear up the confusion that surrounds later comments and the errors that invariably creep into human memory.

Today, Alfred Leete is a rarely-heard name, but a hundred years ago he was one of the great names in an era when illustrators were as well known as the celebrity photographers of today. Daily newspapers had only recently overtaken magazines as the latest mass media. New products and an expanding population to consume them generated the advertising to subsidise the cover prices of these publications. Since 1890, when *London Opinion* achieved half a million sales, weekly magazines had developed mass media business models that paved the way for their owners to create the next mass media, daily tabloid newspapers such as the *Daily Mail, Daily Express* and *Daily Mirror,* between 1896 and 1903.

Media growth was phenomenal. In 1909, the first cinema had been built in Britain and by 1916 twenty million people a year were going to five thousand cinemas. However, even the idea of a national radio had yet to be voiced, never mind television. Telephones were still rare, as were cars. It would be the next world war before the work of

Polish mathematicians, hundreds of code-breakers and scientists such as Alan Turing and Tommy Flowers paved the way for computers with the 'bombes' and electronic digital information processing machines at Bletchley Park. Leo, the world's first office computer, would not be cranked up for Lyons Tea Shops until 1951. Buses were still omnibuses, prams were perambulators and the writers of the day were still more likely to be using a pen than a typewriter. Words and phrases such as 'camouflage', 'over the top' and 'shell-shock' had yet to enter the language; the Zeppelin was still a fantastical form of leisure travel and a tank was something that held water.

Much of our story is played out during the First World War, which soon became known as the Great War. Indeed, the war created this poster, so it is an integral part of the plot. The main military action of that terrible conflict was played out within a strip of land that stretched from just north of Dunkirk on the Channel coast across France to the Swiss border – four hundred miles long, though barely a mile wide in places. The 'trench warfare' began in early 1915 when Sir John French, commander of the 120,000-strong British Expeditionary Force, ordered his men to entrench and the Germans did likewise. For the next three years, the opposing armies faced each other across a blasted strip of earth, keeping their heads down in stinking, rat-infested trenches and living burrowed into the ground. Between 1914 and 1918, some nine million people were slaughtered and up to twenty million injured. Astoundingly, the British army was made up of volunteers for the first two years of the war, and posters were seen as vital to that recruitment effort.

Some 5,704,000 men served in the army during the First World War, compared with 3,788,000 between 1939 and 1945. Perhaps its most remarkable feature was that nearly half of those who filled its ranks between August 1914 and November 1918 were volunteers. By the end of 1915, in fact, 2,466,719 had voluntarily enlisted in the army.

In monetary terms, Britain's national debt multiplied by a factor of eight during the conflict, from £648,000,000 to more than £5,000,000,000. Furthermore, the fighting drained ordinary people's pockets too, as well as their taxes. Within two years of the outbreak of war, food was not scarce, but it was dear – the man in the street saw a near doubling in the cost of essentials, much of the rise being caused by losses of merchant ships to German submarines. In early 1917, the popular Lyons tea shops removed sugar from their tables because it was becoming scarce. Later in the year, the price of bread was subsided and a maximum level set. After various campaigns to encourage people to use food more wisely, dig up their gardens and have 'meatless days', rationing was introduced in the final year of the war.

Initially, cavalry played a part in the fighting. Since the experience of the Boer wars, riders had trained as a highly mobile hybrid force, able to fight on horseback with sword and lance, or ride quickly into battle, dismount and fight as infantry with rifles. In addition to men, millions of horses were vital for transport throughout the conflict. However, this was the first fully modern war, fought between industrialised nations with arsenals of machine guns, long-range artillery, submarines, aircraft, tanks, motorised transport and mass-produced goods. The fighting was reported in the mass media of the day, newspapers and magazines, and documented with photography and cine film. It was the first 'total' war involving whole populations of men, women and children on what came to be called the Home Front as well as soldiers who had volunteered or were conscripted.

The nature of modern warfare was driven home to civilians not only by the number of men who went off to fight but by naval bombardment of coastal towns and then the appearance of Zeppelins over British towns and cities. Although the first Zeppelin was brought down over Belgium in 1915, it would be two years before fighter aircraft were equipped with incendiary bullets to destroy the airships reliably. The raids captured the public's imagination and were regularly depicted in cartoons as a spectacle; later, the Zeppelins were compared critically with the advent of tanks. The airship attacks were replaced by Gotha bombers from 1917. In January 1918, the Odhams printing works in London's Covent Garden was hit in the worst incident of the war. A bomb fell on the pavement and exploded in the basement, which was being used as an air raid shelter. The building collapsed and thirty-eight people were killed and twice as many injured. The government was concerned by the effect on civilian morale – and that of troops overseas worried about their families – so substantial resources were devoted to defences, including searchlights, barrage balloons and anti-aircraft guns as well as fighter aircraft. A lighting black-out was ordered to try to hinder enemy navigation and in London people took to the Underground tunnels as bomb shelters. Most of the attacks, which took place more or less fortnightly throughout the war, were aimed at military or transport targets, but city centres were hit and children were evacuated to the countryside. Such raids were not regarded as a military success, although 1,500 people were killed in the attacks.

Despite the technological developments, the war was waged with nineteenth-century notions and cultural assumptions – most of the soldiers had been born during sixty years of peace in Europe and many had only heard about war from reports about conflicts in far imperial provinces. The Boer War had ended in 1902 and although there had been constant action across the British Empire, these minor wars were fought by volunteer, professional soldiers with the action a long way from the working man in Britain.

Some poignant real images are associated with World War I, though most people are more likely to recall footage from the BBC television series *Blackadder* or more recently Michael Morpurgo's *War Horse* book and the play and film adaptations. While these may give a visual impression of the conditions, they cannot portray the true horror endured by the men who spent weeks at a time in the horrendous conditions that were the reality of the trenches. Conditions so terrible that most men, who as a gender are rarely short of anecdotes about their adventures, could never discuss that period for the rest of their lives. What is most striking today is to visit one of the many cemeteries in Belgium or France – there are almost a thousand sites – with the largest, Tyne Cot near Ypres, holding twelve thousand graves.

The contemporary visions of the war that have survived are black and white cine film of men emerging from the trenches and going 'over the top'. They rush forward into the mist over barbed wire – one falling, presumably killed, another man carries his wounded comrade along a muddy trench. These scenes come from the *Battle of the Somme*, a film produced by the War Propaganda Bureau, which also commissioned work from writers such as Thomas Hardy and H.G. Wells and enlisted the help of newspaper editors. Although much of the film is footage taken on the front line over a fortnight starting in the last week of June 1916, there are many 'staged' sequences filmed in July.

The two cinematographers, Geoffrey Malins and John Benjamin McDowell, operated in different parts of the British army's front line: Malins filming in the vicinity of Beaumont Hamel, about ninety-five miles south-east of Calais; and McDowell working a few miles farther south in the vicinity of Fricourt and Mametz. They returned to France a week later and filmed staged sequences of shellfire and of troops advancing from their trenches at a British Third Army mortar school near St Pol. It is difficult in the film to decide which parts are real and which staged, which should remind us that many of our own memories are second-hand and may not always represent the reality of the time.

One of the most famous events of the war, the 'Christmas truce' of 1914 when soldiers from both sides called unofficial ceasefires on parts of the front, sang carols and even played football, did take place (Figure 2). However, it did not happen all along the battle line. Bill Clarke, a correspondent for the *Daily Mail* who had managed to smuggle himself into the Flanders battle zone despite a government ban on all reporters at the front, reported:

'The Germans came down upon the countryside in a fury of hate, their fiercest onslaught of the week they reserved for Christmas Day ... the guns thumped, the machine guns tapped, and the rifles cracked.

That was the music of Christmas.'

Figure 2. German and British soldiers mingle on Christmas Day 1914

Figure 3. The Irish rebels turned their ire from *John Bull* to the Kaiser Great War?'

Figure 4. The Socialist tiger is harnessed to the nation's needs

Figure 5. A munitions worker seeks her fair return – the vote – from Asquith, the prime minister

Forty years leading up to war

In May 1871, *Blackwood's Edinburgh Magazine* published a short story, *The Battle of Dorking: Reminiscences of a volunteer* that was to influence public debate right up to the start of the Great War and spark a Victorian genre later described as 'scare fiction' and known to academia today as 'invasion literature'. *Blackwood's* was an influential right-wing monthly that specialised in tales of military and colonial life and was sold globally as wel as at home.

Today, *Blackwood's* is probably best known for establishing the careers, among others, of both *Middlemarch* author George Eliot and Joseph Conrad, whose *Heart of Darkness* it serialised in 1899. The initially anonymous *Battle of Dorking* (by army engineer George Tomkyns Chesney) describes how a secret weapon deployed by the Prussians (as today's Germans were then known) destroys the Royal Navy and the ineffective defenders are defeated near Dorking in Surrey. The invading force conquers Britain and the Empire is broken up.

The work sold more than 100,000 copies as a pamphlet and was published in a number of editions as a book and translated into several languages. Such was its influence that William Gladstone, the prime minister, was driven to speak out against it. Four months after the May issue of Blackwood's appeared, army manoeuvres involving 30,000 men were held on the Hog's Back, a ridge between Farnham and Guildford in Surrey. Chesney went on to become a reforming general and was knighted for his work in both Britain and India. For one academic, Patrick Kirkwood:

> '*The Battle of Dorking* was central to the parliamentary, military and public "invasion" controversies of the 1870s. Subsequent developments, ranging from recurring print and parliamentary debates, to military manoeuvres and the eventual building of a series of forts along the North Downs support this position ⋯ *The Battle of Dorking* was equal parts fantasy "invasion literature" and policy document. Its frequent citation by members of both houses of parliament, and by military men engaged in public and private debates, serves to back this claim, as does Chesney's rapid integration into the pro-military reform wing of the Conservative Parliamentary Party of the 1890s.'

Adding to the genre, Liverpool-born journalist Louis Tracy wrote several books about future war, the best known being the 1896 Final War, a book dedicated to 'Private Thomas Atkins' (a nickname for the average British soldier that dates back at least to the time of the Battle of Waterloo – from which we get 'Tommy'). He saw his work as describing 'a great war to be the end of all war' and it ends in victory for the British with the help of the US against the Germans and French. Tracy's books include elements of science fiction, with a Britsh secret weapon, the Thompson Electric Rifle helping ensure victory.

The invasion theme was taken up by H. G. Wells in his War of the Worlds, which was first published in *Pearson's Magazine* in parts from June 1897. For Wells, the enemy comes from another planet and, though the aliens easily overwhelm the defenders, they are ultimately defeated (by nature's bacteria). As with Chesney's book, the Surrey stockbroker belt is pivotal, with the Martians landing on the edge of the town of Woking, just fourteen miles from Dorking.

The more popular penny weekly magazines did not miss out on the invasion theme, with Answers serialising Frederick White's The Lion's Claw, which has the old enemies, the French and Russians, invading, and the next week in 1900, *Pearson's Weekly* putting out 'The Invaders: A story of Britain's peril' by Louis Tracy, with the Germans as the villains of the piece. Three years later, Germany returns as the enemy when a gathering invasion force is discovered in Robert Erskine Childers' Riddle of the Sands.

Ten years after that, in War Inevitable by Alan Burgoyne, an MP who specialised in naval affairs, a fictionalised Lord Kitchener comes to the rescue after German motor torpedo boats devastate the British fleet in a sneak attack. A year before the real war breaks out.

When William Came by 'Saki' (Hector Hugh Munro) was published. This book follows on from Chesney's theme of forty years earlier, describing life under German occupation: the 'William' of the title is Kaiser Wilhelm II – 'Kaiser Bill' to the British people at the time. With the outbreak of the war, a new edition of the Battle of Dorking was published.

Ralph Straus wrote a summary of these 'scare-fictionists' in the second issue of *Bystander* magazine after World War I was declared. The article, 'Armageddon – in prophecy', is illustrated with a painting depicting aerial warfare by Guy Lipscombe from Burgoyne's book. He discusses how 'About the middle of the century Germany definitely emerged to take France's old place as our potential enemy' and describes how such writers 'have come to the truth.'

These fictional works spurred debate in the real world. As the new century began, Britain was the only European power that did not have a large conscript army, even though many prominent figures had been pressing for compulsory military service since the first Boer War. Among these advocates was George Shee, a barrister and Liberal imperialist, who in 1901 published *The Briton's First Duty: The case for conscription* in which he argued for a compulsory home defence army to protect against invasion. Despite the strength of the British navy, it could not guarantee to prevent an invasion force crossing the Channel, only that it would be able to cut its supply lines. Out of the conscription movement came the National Service League in 1902, which from 1905 was led by the Boer War hero Lord Roberts and saw its membership increase from 2,000 to about 95,000 by 1913.

Alongside Lord Roberts's 'crusade' were many patriotic leagues, among which can be counted Baden-Powell's Boy Scouts – who played a role in civil defence during the war, guarding the water supply system, running patrols from groups of twenty or thirty scouts attached to city police stations and sounding the 'all clear' on their bugles after air raids. The influence of such patriotic leagues was such that a large percentage of youngsters had been engaged in physical activity and were trained in some kind of uniformed organisation by the time war broke out.

Britain's foreign policy changed direction during the first few years of the new century. Remember that for this generation, the Battle of Waterloo and Wellington's final victory over Napoleon's French armies, with help from Prussian (German) forces under Blucher, was as close in time as the Great War is to us today. In his compilation of reports from the *Daily Mail*, Twells Brex dates the start of the falling out to 1864, when British sympathy for Denmark in the Schleswig-Holstein campaign aroused the resentment of the Prussians, as did England's neutrality during the Franco-German war of 1870. Such was the feeling in Germany that Brex quotes a British ambassador saying 'it might take generations to allay the vindictiveness of the German people'.

After the Jameson raid in South Africa in 1896, the Kaiser had sent a telegram to President Kruger congratulating the Boer action against 'armed bands, which invaded your country as disturbers of the peace'. In 1900, the German navy laws saw a great expansion in the number of warships. This military expansion was interpreted as being against Britain, and Germany had made no secret of its support for the Boers, so British thinking switched. In the Edwardian era, instead of the traditional cordiality towards Germany and fear of a combined France and Russia, the nation became friendly towards France and Russia and hostile to Germany.

An Anglo-French agreement in 1904, mainly over their respective interests in Egypt and Morocco, alarmed the Germans. The question arose of what would be Britain's response should Germany attack France over a dispute about Morocco. The answer can be found in the summer manoeuvres of the English army at the time, which assumed that Germany, not France, would be the enemy. Germany also felt humiliated by the Treaty of Algeciras, which temporarily settled the Morocco dispute, and felt surrounded by hostile powers, a feeling that grew alarmingly after an Anglo-Russian entente in 1906. The result was a naval arms race based on ever more powerful dreadnoughts. World War I broke out in August 1914, when Germany declared war on Russia. Trouble in the Balkans precipitated the outbreak of hostilities, but they had been brewing for a long time.

Whether in fiction, or the real world, war came to be seen as inevitable for many people and the most likely enemy was Germany.

Figure 6. A Tommy reflects

Figure 7. Tom Browne cartoon of
Kitchener as the music hall star
Chirgwin

Figure 8. Last photograph of Kitchener
alive aboard the Hampshire (June
1916)

Figure 9. How Bernard Partridge
marked the loss of Kitchener in *Punch*

The Edwardian social scene

King George V came to the throne in 1910, the son of King Edward VII and Alexandra of Denmark, a sister to the empress of Russia. In 1893, George had married Princess Victoria Mary of Teck (a town in modern-day Germany) who had been engaged to his brother. The marriage was a success and George, unlike his father, never took a mistress. They had six children, Edward, Albert, Mary, Henry, George and John. They lived on the Sandringham estate in Norfolk and it was George who changed his family name from the German Saxe-Coburg-Gotha to that of Windsor in 1917 as a response to anti-German public sentiment. Alongside Mary, known as 'May', George reigned until his death in 1935.

The royal family had close ties to their Central European cousins but most working people would have had little contact with anyone outside their country, or even outside their immediate area. The motor-car and the telephone were still rarities, though the bicycle was revolutionising personal transport, while the idea of a BBC radio broadcast was yet to become a dream.

For the urban working classes, the music hall was the great entertainment, which provides an idea of the morality of the times and the great divide between the royal circle and the people. The most popular artiste of the day was the twice-divorced Marie Lloyd but she was not invited to perform in the first Royal Variety Performance in 1912 – because she was regarded as too risqué to appear before George V and Queen Mary. Fans savoured the double entendres of her songs such as 'I sits among the cabbages and peas.'

At the international level, the balance of power was shifting. In Europe, the decisive factor was the rise of a united Germany, while across the Atlantic the United States was expanding quickly. Britain was still emerging from the glories and certainty of the Victorian era with class distinctions very much a way of life. These distinctions can be seen in the magazines people read, such as the *Queen* – which was launched by Samuel Beaton with the permission of Victoria in 1867 and published Mrs Beaton's recipes – costing a shilling a copy. Other popular titles included the six-penny *Tatler*, *Bystander* and *Punch* through to the penny weeklies *John Bull*, *Pearson's*, Answers and *London Opinion*. Somewhere in between was *London Opinion*, a title that has disappeared from common recognition, but was then a thriving success and plays a vital role in our tale.

The image of the aristocracy portrayed in their magazines was one of splendid and carefree easy living, but this was a contrast to the forces of discontent and resentment felt by many other members of society. In particular, resentment among the working classes ran deep. In 1900, massive costs had been levied against the trade unions after a legal judgment in favour of the owners of the Taff Vale railway and this was the catalyst for the creation of a political party that supported the trade unions. Initially called the Labour Representative Committee in 1906, it became the Labour Party. The two established parties were the Conservatives and the Liberals. And it was a Liberal chancellor of the exchequer, the Welshman David Lloyd George, who pushed through a 'people's budget' in 1909 that proposed an income tax on the rich to pay for reforms, the introduction of social insurance and the rebuilding of the Royal Navy.

The rise of such men as Lloyd George from humble origins to high positions in the government showed the changing nature of political life, a change that the House of Lords was slow to accept. The upper house, packed with hereditary peers, considered the people's budget to be a socialist project and rejected it. Two general elections were held to resolve the deadlock with the Liberals finally winning a landslide victory. In the interim, the Lords continued to reject the budget, which was finally passed in 1911 when the Commons approved the Parliament Act to limit the delaying power of the House of Lords. From then on, the Lords could no longer reject bills outright and there was to be a general election every five years (instead of seven). The Liberals remained in power until a wartime coalition government was formed in 1915.

August 1911 saw great industrial unrest. Strikes of dockworkers, railwaymen and miners brought the country to a standstill. The government was forced to respond. The National Insurance Act was passed to ensure that the worker, the employer and the government all contributed to a general fund to pay for free medical treatment, sick pay, disability and maternity benefits. It also introduced a measure of unemployment benefits, and free meals for school children as well as periodic medical examinations. Through the efforts of Winston Churchill, labour exchanges were set up where unemployed workers could sign on for vacant jobs. Foundations were being laid for a sea change in the state's responsibility for the welfare of its citizens. Although there were strikes through the war, they were few and far between.

That same year, Irish MPs who had helped the Liberals gain power wanted their reward in home rule. To the Conservatives, however, the idea of Britain splitting up (in the face of a hostile Germany) seemed ludicrous, to be avoided at all costs. They were aided by the Protestant forces of Ulster, equally alarmed at the prospect of being ruled from Dublin. Civil war loomed in Ireland, and the British army regulars made it clear in the so-called 'mutiny' at the Curragh, that they would not fight against their brothers in Ulster. The outbreak of war totally altered Irish attitudes. The suddenness of the change was summarised in a *Bystander* cartoon of 19 August 1914 by Francis Rigney, 'The change in Ireland' (Figure 3).

Three frames show an Ulster Volunteer and a Nationalist Volunteer both about to start a fight with John Bull over home rule, when the Kaiser approaches in a boat – and they both head off to battle the invader! 'Of all the impudence – let me at him' cries one; 'Will you do me a favour John? Just let me get one clout,' cries the other as John Bull looks on nonplussed. In September, the Home Rule Bill was finally pushed through, though its implementation was delayed and the island was not divided until 1920.

It can never be known what would have happened in the workplace and in Ireland had hostilities not begun in Europe in the summer of 1914. Statistics show the level of industrial discontent at the time. In 1911, 9 per cent of the total industrial population was involved in strikes, compared with 2.6 per cent for 1902, 1.4 per cent for 1907, and an average of 2.9 per cent for the period.

Yet, a *London Opinion* cartoon by Bert Thomas, 'The tolerated tiger', eight months into the war shows a tiger marked 'Socialism' hauling a cart of provisions for a soldier off to war (Figure 4). An onlooking figure representing capitalism comments:

'To think I should have lived to approve the harnessing of the Socialist tiger to the nation's needs.'

Another area of strife that was calmed was the fight for women's suffrage, a battle that Emmeline Pankhurst had been waging for twenty-five years. Such was her famed determination that a colour postcard shows a saluting officer telling Kitchener:

'My Lord, it is reported that the Germans are going to disembark at Dover!'

Kitchener, in full uniform with a quill pen in his hand and a map of the empire marked in pink on his desk, replies:

'Very Well! 'phone Mrs Pankhurst to go there with some suffragettes, and that will do!'

Her Votes for Women campaign was called off and women were desperately needed in munitions factories. However, the suffragettes' did not go away. Kitchener received a Suffragist deputation at the War Office in January 1915, for example, demanding that arbitrary restrictions should not be imposed on soldiers' wives by commanding officers, such as not being served in hotels and public houses after six in the evening. Women from the landed gentry would soon find themselves working alongside working class women. By mid-1916, it was estimated that 766,000 women had replaced men in civil employment alone, and many more had taken up work in munitions factories and other occupations that the war had generated, with their voluminous initials such as WAACs, VADs, WRNSs and WRAFs.

There was a certain thrill to the sight of women in everyday men's jobs, as *Times* journalist Michael MacDonagh later recalled in his published diaries, he remarks that:

'On seeing his first policewoman in her 'dowdy uniform, sex keeps breaking through in bright eyes, shapely ankles and ripe red lips … a susceptible lad might well be tempted to commit an offence for the delight of being led captive – abducted, in fact – by one of these fair damsels … The hall-porter at some of the big hotels is an Amazon in blue or mauve coat, gold-braided peaked cap and high top-boots – a gorgeous figure that fascinates me. But my favourite is the young "conductorette" on trams and buses, in her smart jacket, short skirt to the knees and leather leggings.'

Some 260,000 women ultimately formed the Land Army, three times as many women as were working on farms at the war's start. There was even a magazine, the *Landwoman*, to promote the movement. At the outbreak of the war, women did not have the right to vote but those aged thirty won the vote in 1918, though it was another decade before equal voting rights with men at twenty-one came in (Figure 5).

This was very different age to live in. The working man 'knew his place'. Living conditions were poor and life expectancy was forty-six for men and fifty for women (seventy-seven and eighty-one today). One in three children under the age of five died, compared with fewer than one in a hundred today. The cause of death was often respiratory, infectious and parasitic diseases rather than today's cancer, heart disease and stroke. One wonders just how many men were motivated to join the army in 1914 as a chance of escaping this drab existence rather than out of patriotic fervour, little knowing that the glamour of enlistment would rapidly evolve into the horrors of trench warfare (Figure 6).

The Great War

The war was a terrible experience for all involved. Within a muddy, shell-torn strip of land, men burrowed to escape the shelling and moved around in trenches for four years. The exceptions were a few generals and their staffs, comfortably billeted miles behind the lines. Some of them never even visited the trenches, such was the reality of military life at the time. On all sides, some seventy million men were mobilised, nine million of them were killed and up to twenty million injured.

The war consumed huge quantities of both men and materials – which the protagonists had to organise, often to the cost of other national requirements. Lord Kitchener saw what was coming and set out to expand the British army from its relatively small size of 730,000 officers and men, just one-third of whom were regulars and the rest in reserve formations, the Territorials. Most officers came from public schools with the rank and file being labourers. Kitchener's strategy employed state-of-the-art marketing techniques to attract volunteers. However, the high casualty rates on the Western Front led to a sharp fall in volunteers so two Military Service Acts were passed in 1916 that meant all British men were eligible for conscription.

The conflict was triggered by the assassination of Archduke Franz Ferdinand, heir to the throne of Austria-Hungary, on 28 June 1914. Within weeks, the major powers were at war and, via their colonies, the conflict spread around the globe. The Austro-Hungarians fired the first shots and, while the Russians mobilised, the Germans invaded neutral Belgium and Luxembourg on the way to France. Berlin's attack led to Britain's declaration of war against Germany. Japan was a British ally and seized German possessions in the Pacific and East Asia. After the German march was brought to a halt by the French with the help of the British Expeditionary Force just fifty kilometres from Paris – the 'Miracle of the Marne' – the Western Front settled into a static battle of attrition with a trench line that changed little until 1917.

After a 1918 German offensive, the Allies drove back the Germans and US forces began entering the trenches. Germany agreed to an armistice on 11 November 1918. The war ended in victory for the Allies. The result was that four imperial powers – the German, Russian, Austro-Hungarian and Ottoman (Turkish) empires – ceased to exist.

By war's end, of the seventy million military personnel mobilised, including sixty million Europeans, one in ten had died. The fact that so many were killed was largely due to the technological advancements that led to enormous increases in the lethality of weapons without corresponding improvements in protection or mobility. The conflict paved the way for many political changes, even revolutions in some of the nations involved.

In his book *Eleventh Month, Eleventh Day, Eleventh Hour*, Joseph Persico tells how, on the final day before eleven o'clock, thousands of German soldiers were massacred and nearly 11,000 on both sides needlessly wounded by the actions of allied soldiers thrown into frantic action by generals who already knew that an armistice had been signed – more on this single day than the total killed, wounded or missing on D-Day almost twenty-seven years later.

Among the German soldiers wounded was a corporal, Adolf Hitler, who lived to fight another day because of the compassion of a British private, Henry Tandey. The story, which has various versions, goes that Hitler was wounded in hand-to-hand fighting at Marcoing, near Cambrai, and Tandey refused to shoot the injured enemy soldier at point blank range. Tandey had earlier been in an incident that led to his receiving a Victoria Cross for rescuing a wounded comrade during the battle at Menin crossroads. The incident was made the subject of a painting by Fortunino Matania, an Italian artist regarded as one of the best of his generation who lived in London and worked for the *Illustrated London News*.

Tandey was a highly decorated soldier, being awarded a Distinguished Conduct Medal as well as the VC. Fifteen years later, when Hitler became German chancellor, he requested a print of the painting, which was owned by the Green Howards. The regiment sent a print to the Führer, who put it on show at his mountain retreat at Berchtesgaden. Hitler had apparently recognised the British soldier from Matania's painting in a newspaper cutting but the story did not come out until it was recounted to Tandey by British prime minister Neville Chamberlain. On one of Chamberlain's trips to Germany that resulted in the signing of the ill-fated Munich Agreement in 1938, Hitler had shown him the print and told him that it was of the soldier who had spared his life two decades earlier. Something else that Hitler gained an admiration for was the way in Britain 'propaganda was considered a weapon of the first order.' He also wrote in Mein Kampf, of the 'unheard-of skill and ingenious deliberation' that was applied and said that: 'At the beginning it was apparently crazy in the impudence of its assertions, later it became disagreeable, and finally it was believed. After four and a half years a revolution broke out in Germany the slogan of which came from the enemy's war propaganda.'

Figure 10. 'Paysage aux affinches' by Pablo Picasso (1912)

Figure 11. Advertisement for Dada hair

Figure 12. One of the first recruiting posters

Figure 13. 'Remember Scarborough' from the PRC. Note the reference to 'German barbarians'

Kitchener – the man

Horatio Herbert Kitchener was the most famous military man of his day. Born on 24 June 1850 in County Kerry, Ireland, he was educated in Switzerland and at the Royal Military Academy in Woolwich In 1871, he joined the Royal Engineers. By the turn of the century his face was not only portrayed in newspapers and magazines, but on postcards, cartoons, badges, photographs for the home, cigarette cards, matchboxes and pottery – and he was even sold in the form of several dolls – the world's first Action Man! The pocket-sized *Kitchener Birthday Book* issued in 1916 printed an event in K.K.'s life, or a saying he had made, for every day of the year. Paintings by R. Canton Woodville and Dudley Hardy portray him at key stages in his life: in Arab dress, in Egypt, in the ruins of Khartoum, at the Durbar in Delhi, on the Western Front and at Gallipoli.

Even in the great entertainment venues, the music halls, such was his popularity that Ludwig Amann, billed as 'The Greatest Facial Artiste of the Age' who used lightning-fast make-up changes to mimic famous faces, portrayed Kitchener along with Napoleon, Gladstone and the king. In another entertainment reference that probably contrasted Kitchener's dour demeanour with the joviality of a performer, he was drawn by cartoonist Tom Browne as a music hall star, George H. Chirgwin, whose sentimental song 'Blind Boy' was a favourite with audiences. Chirgwin performed with a blacked-up face with a diamond-shaped 'white eye' and had long been billed as 'The White-Eyed Kaffir'. The term 'Kaffir' had not yet gained today's racist meaning of the Apartheid era in South Africa, originally describing the Bantu ethnic group. However, it was in currency as a term for a white man who adopted the habits of native tribes, and Kitchener may have been seen in this light, in learning Arabic and in the brutal way he behaved in his campaigns. The decapitating of the rebel leader, the Mahdi, was described by the Guardian:

> 'It is, we believe, quite 'exceptional' for a British general to insult a dead body. These things are done by savages, but they hardly form a suitable beginning for the lessons in civilisation which we are to teach the Soudanese.'

A more obvious comparison was height, with Chirgwin wearing a skin-tight black costume, tall hat and very long shoes. So, the stern, tall general in Browne's hands became 'Mr Bert Kitchener the Popular White-Eyed Kaffir of the Oxford Music Hall.' The subject is drawn as too tall for the page, with the legs below the knees shown in a separate frame, and the feet so large they break out of that second frame (Figure 7).

Kitchener's glaring, unsmiling stare was well known to the public. On one of the rare occasions he was photographed smiling and the

21

image published as a postcard, the caption was: 'Lord Kitchener smiles.' His hobby was collecting Chinese porcelain and he had 'the eye of a mandarin for the rare beauties of the art of the East', according to an article in the Sphere.

Kitchener's military reputation was formed out in the empire: South Africa, India and Egypt. He had served with the Royal Engineers from 1871, doing survey work in Palestine and Cyprus, before becoming military vice-consul at Erzerum in eastern Turkey in 1879. Three years later he took control of the Egyptian cavalry, became Sirdar (commander-in-chief of the army) and stayed on in the region until 1898 when he was made a peer. Then followed three years in South Africa and seven years in India as commander-in-chief. In 1911, when he returned to Egypt as agent-general, a *Punch* cartoon by W.H. Townsend depicted him on horseback returning the stare of the Sphinx with the caption: 'Kindred spirits.' Kitchener stood a ramrod-straight six feet two inches (1.88 metres) tall at a time when the average height of a recruit would have been five feet and five inches (1.65m).

To the Fleet Street newspapers and magazines, Kitchener was the hero who had crushed the Mahdist rebellion at Omdurman after the rebels had beheaded General Charles 'Chinese' Gordon in the days when Victoria was still on the throne. Gordon's final moments were depicted in a heroic 1893 painting, the 'Siege of Khartoum' by George W. Joy.

A 1966 film, *Khartoum*, starring Charlton Heston as Gordon and Laurence Olivier as the Mahdi, the rebel leader, revived the scene shown in the painting of the general facing death on a staircase. Peter Arne played a young Major Kitchener. As well as being called the 'Avenger of Gordon', Kitchener was known as 'Kitchener of Khartoum', a title he adopted on being made a viscount in 1902, or simply 'K of K'. He was caricatured for an 1899 issue of *Vanity Fair* as simply 'Khartoum' by 'Spy' (the nom de crayon of Sir Leslie Ward). For a whole front-page page portrait in the Graphic in 1915, he was 'A man with an iron will'.

Kitchener's exploits were widely reported internationally and many books were written about him and his campaigns, which were published in both Britain and the US. His arrival back in Dover from South Africa in November 1898 was marked with a full-page painting in the *London Illustrated News*, for example, and his return to Southampton in July 1902 was front page news in the US for *Boston's Sunday Herald*, with the headline 'A great hero is Kitchener'. The books included *With Kitchener in the Soudan*, by the popular adventure novelist George Henty, as well as biographies and military history.

New technology was a feature often reported in the press, and not just for weaponry: the use of heliographs for communications was an innovation in the Zulu wars for example. Postcards would show Kitchener alongside images of aircraft, dreadnoughts and giant artillery pieces. Among the books about these conflicts was *With Kitchener's*

Army by Owen Watkins, an army chaplain, the frontispiece of which shows the latest in medical technology – a portable X-ray machine being use at Abadieh Hospital in the Sudan. A street running past the cathedral in Port Said was named after Kitchener; an island in the Nile; the Indian army still occupies Kitchener House in Kolkata (Calcutta); and shortly after his death the Canadian city of Berlin changed its name to Kitchener.

The general had a stormy relationship with journalists, but the war correspondent G.W. Steevens built the foundation for Kitchener's reputation with his Boer War reports in the *Daily Mail* and his book, With Kitchener to Khartoum. Yet Steevens was also aware of the faults of the man who came up with the idea of concentration camps to hold prisoners, describing him as 'more a machine than man. You feel that he ought to be patented and shown with pride at the Paris International Exhibition. British Empire: Exhibit No. 1, hors concours, the Sudan Machine.' Steevens went on: 'He would be a splendid manager of the War Office. He would be a splendid manager of anything.' Prophetic words from a book published in 1898.

Even Kitchener's most sympathetic biographers made no attempts to conceal that he was perceived as a distant, stern and sometimes ruthless figure – although they claimed that the real man was less inaccessible than he seemed. Many politicians were critical of Kitchener, especially Winston Churchill, who had served under him in the Sudan, while doubling up as a war correspondent. Henry Davray quotes Churchill's words from his own book, *The River War*, about the 1898 campaign to gain control of the Nile:

> 'The general [Kitchener] who never spared himself cared little for others. He treated all men like machines, from the private soldier whose salutes he disdained, to the superior officers he rigidly controlled. The comrade who had served with him and under him for many years in peace and peril was flung aside incontinently as soon as he ceased to be of use. The Sirdar looked only to the soldiers who could march and fight ⋯ the victories which marked the progress of the River War were accompanied by acts of barbarity not always justified even by the harsh customs of savage conflicts or the fierce and treacherous nature of the Dervish.'

However, he shared his first name, Horatio, with Nelson and inspired a Nelsonian confidence among the public, despite having no experience of modern European warfare, little knowledge of the British army at home, or the War Office – and no experience of Westminster politics. At the outbreak of war, such was Kitchener's reputation that Herbert Asquith, the prime minister, was pressed to bring in the governor of Egypt as secretary of war. Lord Northcliffe, the owner of the *Times* who had made his fortune with *Answers* magazine and *Comic Cuts* and gone on to launch the *Daily Mail* (1896) and the *Daily Mirror* (1903), wanted the sixty-four-year-old Kitchener in the post – and the Northcliffe newspapers had influence. 'A harsh, ruthless, implacable soldier' he may have been, but Kitchener was also lauded as a skilful military organiser. In an editorial discussing the merits of Kitchener and Lord Haldane, the chancellor, Northcliffe's *Times* of 5 August thundered:

> 'The eve of battle is the time for plain words. We object to the selection of Lord Haldane for the War Office because, in our belief, and in the belief of the enormous majority of his countrymen, he is not the best man available for the post. The best man in unquestionably Lord Kitchener, whose long and varied experience of the work of organising warfare is unequalled among British soldiers.'

The *Times* headline on page six the next day was 'New war minister. Lord Kitchener appointed'. However, Kitchener seems not to have wanted the job and tried to return to Egypt. The prime minister, Asquith, had to call him back. On 4 August, Britain had declared war on Germany without a secretary of war in place, but the Avenger of Gordon now had the job.

The *Times* journalist Michael MacDonagh witnessed Kitchener's speech in the House of Lords on 25 August 1914, saying it was 'characteristic of Kitchener's aloofness and isolation' that he should come in unaccompanied and unobtrusively, only to take a place on the bench where the bishops sat. However, MacDonagh was 'taken by the shy, diffident and sunny relaxation' of Kitchener's smile when he was told he was in the wrong place. Kitchener wore glasses to read his statement, the delivery of which was 'unimpressive' and 'He appeared to be in a hurry to get the ordeal over and done with.'

Kitchener's record as secretary of state for war was mixed. A nickname coined in South Africa, when as chief of staff he had broken up the regimental system of transport and supply and initially been dubbed 'K of Chaos', resurfaced because Kitchener's Army and the Territorial Army both competed for volunteers and equipment. While Kitchener's recruitment campaign was a swift success, he was blamed for a shortage of high explosive shells at Ypres in May 1915.

The Northcliffe papers turned on their early favourite over the shells crisis and became the war minister's prime critics. The headline 'Need for shells' with subsidiary decks such as 'British attacks checked. Limited supply the cause' in the *Times* was mild, though repeated over several days, compared with the *Daily Mail* a week later: 'The shells scandal. Lord Kitchener's tragic blunder. Our terrible casualty list.' Added pressure from other newspapers and campaigning magazines such as *John Bull* – whose editor Horatio Bottomley could fill London's Albert Hall with his lectures – led to the formation of a coalition government and Kitchener lost control over munitions and strategy.

However, in his biography of Kitchener, Philip Magnus describes how readers turned against the newspapers because the attack on 'the nation's idol caused widespread dismay and indignation'. Copies of the Mail were burnt outside the London Stock Exchange, subscriptions were cancelled in the gentlemen's clubs of St. James's and Pall Mall, but the press attacks continued. Ultimately, though, Northcliffe had 'underestimated ⋯ the love and loyalty of the man in the street that Kitchener commanded' and falling sales forced the end of the press campaign. In June of the next year, Kitchener's critics in the Commons attacked him for failing to foresee the need for munitions and not proposing conscription. He faced them up in a private meeting – as a lord he could not appear before MPs in their house – and was able to repel their attacks.

Just four days later, the *Evening News* headline at lunchtime on 6 June was: 'Lord Kitchener drowned.' Kitchener had sailed for Russia aboard HMS Hampshire to persuade the tsar to continue fighting the Germans (Figure 8.). However, the cruiser had to take shelter in a storm and sank. The official line was that the ship had been struck by a torpedo or a floating mine. By the evening, rumours were circulating that the news was a ruse to mislead the Germans. However, Kitchener's body was never found and stories spread about his death and the mission.

The front page of the *Daily Mirror* for 7 June was a 'Lord Kitchener Memorial Number' with a head-and-shoulders portrait of the 'great field-marshal' taking up almost the whole front page. In the US, the *New York Times* on the same day ran the sinking on its front page with a photograph of Kitchener. The main headline read: 'Kitchener and staff perish at sea; lost on cruiser, perhaps torpedoed; England suspects spies of the deed.'

Among the dozen subsidiary lines were: 'Intern aliens, British cry,' 'London newspapers sure Germans knew of war chief's plans,' 'And sunk the Hampshire,' and 'Northcliffe papers, once earl's opponents, join in the chorus of praise.'

There were some reports of locals being prevented by troops from trying to rescue the few survivors – just a dozen from more than six hundred and fifty officers and men on board. Disturbing questions abounded. Had Kitchener even been on board? Where was the £2 million in gold bullion that was being taken to persuade the tsar? Was it an IRA bomb? Or the work of a Boer spy? It was proposed in parliament that the survivors should face a court-martial to try to answer the 'many questions disturbing the public mind'.

Messages from foreign governments paid tribute to 'one of Britain's most famous sons ⋯ one of the most striking figures of our age'; 'the Great Reformer of the glorious English army'; and 'the brilliant organiser of the mighty British army'. The king and queen attended a memorial service at St Paul's Cathedral along with the prime minister and four thousand mourners. The Sphere devoted seven pages to the service. Leading cartoonist Bernard Partridge marked the loss of Kitchener in *Punch* (Figure 9).

Recruitment advertising chief Sir Hedley Le Bas was appointed to run a national memorial fund with the proceeds going to disabled officers and men. Le Bas also edited the *Lord Kitchener Memorial Book*, which included Kitchener's speeches, along with portraits, cartoons and illustrations, and the signatures of the great and good.

The memorial issue of the *Sphere* summarised a *Daily News* article that described Kitchener as a soldier:

'His methods were patient and laborious rather than swift and empirical. He was not seen at his best on the field of battle or in handling a sudden situation, but in laying his plans for an assured though undramatic end. He realised the magnitude of the war at the beginning with more certainty perhaps than anyone else. Wherever his judgment was brought to bear on the crucial operations of the war it was rarely at fault. It was on his survey of the theatre of war in Gallipoli that the decision to evacuate was taken ⋯ his decision rescued us from an impossible situation and saved the army of Gallipoli.'

His passing inspired the poet Anita Dudley to produce a book of sonnets to Kitchener. Her introduction talks of 'hero worship' and how the news she heard at the Caledonian Market in North London 'came like a thief in the night, whispered from stall to stall by white-faced girls'. She saw how the silence that descended on the raucous market became an 'eloquent tribute' and gave the poet 'her first insight into the heart of the great loving people'. Stall-holders wept, women sobbed aloud and tears rolled down sailors' cheeks before the crowd broke out singing 'Rule Britannia' and 'God Save the King'.

Arguments about Kitchener rumbled on for years and he was criticised by Lord Esher in *The Tragedy of Lord Kitchener*, the essence of the biography being that Kitchener had been called upon to do work for which he was not fit and that 'the armour of his soul had rusted'. This prompted Asquith, the former prime minister who had appointed Kitchener, to leap to his defence in two substantial articles in *Pearson's Magazine* to set out 'the incalculable services which Lord Kitchener rendered to his country in the Great War' and deny Escher's claims. The second article also reproduced a pivotal letter that Kitchener had written to Asquith before the shells crisis, in which he wrote that Field Marshal John French, who commanded the British Expeditionary Force, had told him his troops had as much ammunition as they would need.

It would be easy, from much of the published material on Kitchener, not to warm to him as a person and, indeed, his reputation declined after the 1920s. However, we must consider who was writing about him and their motivation and circumstances. He was undoubtedly a stern and in some ways ruthless officer who was not close to his subordinates but that must be considered with regard to the era. There was, however, another side to him that has rarely been revealed before and that is his relationship with his own family and with members of the opposite sex. In an interview with one of the authors, Lady Kenya Tatton-Brown (née Kitchener in 1923), a great niece of 'our' Kitchener and sister to the late Earl Kitchener of Khartoum, was keen to reject some of the adverse characteristics attributed to him contending that he had a very likeable side, particularly within his own family. She revealed that in diaries kept by Kitchener's nieces (which are still in existence) their uncle was described as being 'great fun'. Moreover, family records of him as a young man on holiday in France dispel any later rumours that he was unable to form relationships with members of the opposite sex.

In a strange twist, in October 1925 the journalist Frank Power began a series of articles in the *Referee,* a Sunday newspaper, questioning events on board the Hampshire at the time Kitchener died. He continued his claims for a number of weeks and the reaction of the public to his claims forced an enquiry by the government, which, apparently, interviewed many people about their recollection of events. The information collected was published a year later. Power then changed his line, claiming Kitchener's body had been found in Norway. He went there with a film crew and a few weeks later a coffin arrived at Waterloo station in London, where Power went to meet it. At this stage, the authorities intervened and the coffin was opened in the presence of the police and Sir Bernard Spilsbury, the forensic scientist who had helped convict the murderer Dr Crippen. The coffin was empty, and it was later shown that Power had engaged in an elaborate hoax. The *Referee* disowned Power, who was interviewed several times by the police, but not prosecuted.

Kitchener's great – and crucial – contribution to Britain's war effort was his foresight in preparing for a long war and driving through a policy of recruiting a large army quickly. He died before his New Army was tested in the Battle of the Somme and so was not associated with his 'lions' being led by 'donkeys' into the slaughter on the Western Front.

Figure 14. 'Daddy, what did YOU do in the Great War?'

Figure 15. Women of Britain say 'GO!'

Figure 16. *Bystander* cartoon of 1914 harks back to a 20-year-old *Punch* cartoon by John Tenniel

Figure 17. Bruce Bairnsfather's first Old Bill cartoon, drawn 'under somewhat difficult circumstances'

The poster in a consumer society

Posters belong to a body of fleeting ephemera. Produced by advertising agencies, government departments, companies and individuals, they are circulated en masse. As Martin Hardie, keeper of prints and drawings at the Victoria and Albert Museum, has noted: 'In its brief existence a poster is battered by the rain and faded by the sun, then pasted over by another message more urgent still.' But the idea of the poster has an ancient history. The walls of Pompeii, the Roman city buried by ash from Vesuvius almost two thousand years ago, are covered to this day with painted messages and advertisements. Bills announcing theatrical events and official statements were stuck to the posts that marked pedestrian routes down London's streets before the Great Fire of 1666, hence the terms 'billposters' and 'billstickers'.

Large typographic posters were common on the walls of European cities by the seventeenth century and with the invention of lithography around 1790, it became much cheaper to reproduce a graphic image on paper. As in Pompeii, the typographical announcements of the Georgian and early Victorian eras were simply pasted up on any suitable surface (hopefully, covering the offerings of a competitor!).

Charles Dickens was one of the first people to use the word 'poster' in print, in *Nicholas Nickelby*, which was published in monthly parts in 1838 and 1839. This world of fly-posting was reined in from the 1860s with the advent of special sites to rent for posters – billposting stations or hoardings. Hoardings, which were erected around the many building sites of the time, were rented by billposters from the site owners. This innovation was promoted by the Bill-Posters' Association founded in 1861 and the Billposter, a trade magazine. It was the start of 'billsticking' becoming 'outdoor advertising'.

Dickens did not live to see the advent of the 'people's picture gallery' that decorated the streets in the late Victorian era. In the days of *Nicholas Nickelby*, colour printing would have been achieved by several wood blocks but chromolithography brought colour printing into the machine age and large posters became common on Victorian streets. Printers and advertisers co-operated to standardise sizes and outdoor displays. The advertising industry itself expanded from the establishment of R.F. White and Son in 1800, with advertising copywriter Eric Field reckoning that 'the *Times* had on its books nearly one hundred advertising agents' by 1895.

The paths of advertising and art crossed continuously in this period. Artists influenced advertising, which – being so widespread – affected their work in return. In the mid-1800s, art shook off tradition and went out into the street, creating advertising through commission and, occasionally, unwillingly. The most famous example of the unexpected advertising illustrator is provided by the painting '*Bubbles*' by the Pre-Raphaelite painter John Everett Millais. Large colour prints of this were first distributed with the Christmas 1887 issue of *Illustrated London News*. Later, with the addition of a bar of soap, it was turned into an advertisement for A&F Pears, a landmark use that helped earn managing director Thomas Barrett a reputation as 'the father of modern advertising'.

The advent of the British graphical poster is dated to 1871, with a dramatic woodcut by the painter and illustrator Fred Walker for a stage version of Wilkie Collins's. In fact, he is often credited with having started the fashion for artistic advertising in Britain.

Martin Hardie, keeper of prints and drawings at the Victoria and Albert Museum, in his introduction to the catalogue for a 1931 exhibition of international posters at the museum, identifies several stages in the development of the poster, with the French next taking on the mantle through Jules Chéret, establishing the affiche artistique (artistic poster) in the 1870s, followed by Henri de Toulouse-Lautrec, Pierre Bonnard and Edouard Vuillard through to the 1890s.

Back in Britain, William Nicholson and James Pryde – working together under the name J. & W. Beggarstaff – brought in a Japanese influence with a definite pattern and restricted, simplified colour. And the work of Aubrey Beardsley 'bore the touch of genius', so that by the end of the century, posters were not only a mature marketing tool, but were collected and recognised as an artistic medium. In 1894-96, two exhibitions of posters were held in London's Royal Aquarium and magazines devoted to poster art were published in the UK, US and France, with titles such as *Studio*, the *Yellow Book* and the *Poster* (1898-1900) promoting the medium.

In the Edwardian era, the expansion of travel by rail, Underground, sea and air provided the wherewithal for the transport poster, such as John Hassall's 'Skegness is So Bracing' of 1908. By 1912, such was the ubiquity of posters that Pablo Picasso was inspired to paint '*Paysage aux affinches*' – 'Landscape with posters' (Figure 10). Leading up to the war, publicity manager Frank Pick was instrumental in driving visual quality on the London Underground. The V&A has described how 'he refused to hang the PRC's posters in his stations because of their poor design.' Instead, he commissioned Frank Brangwyn and Gerald Spencer Pryse.'

The US-born artist Edward McKnight Kauffer, who worked in France and Germany before coming to London at the start of the war, produced well over a hundred designs for London Transport, starting in 1915 when Pick commissioned him to do four landscape posters, including '*Oxhey Wood*' and '*In Watford*'. His painterly style at this stage suggests the influences of both Van Gogh and also of Japanese colour woodcuts, and he later developed an abstract feel. Hardie makes the point that British posters were generally of a far better technical quality than those on the Continent and that in lettering, 'the British poster is still supreme'.

Around the same time, but in Germany, a group of artists were on their way to launching a protest group, their manifesto supposedly inspired by an advertisement for Dada, a hair tonic: Dadaism was born (Figure 11). The group was rebelling against the bourgeois values of the time and giving vent to their despair over futility of war. They had no unifying artistic style, but worked in collage, photomontage and with found objects, rather than traditional forms such as painting and sculpture. (Another version of events is that one of them thrust a knife into a dictionary that stabbed the French word dada, meaning 'hobby-horse'.)

It follows that by 1914, the poster was ready for a propaganda role in time of war (Figure 12). Yet, despite their influence on how many people experienced the war, very few actual posters from the Great War were collected and saved. Most of the images were soon forgotten. Before the Great War it would have been easy to differentiate between a commercial advert and a government one, but during the war it became rapidly less so. Commercial advertising even started to mirror government advertising in the design and wording of posters. At first, many officials objected to the use of posters in war advertising and the deployment of official information. However mass-produced, full colour, large format posters could be considered an innovation of warfare, the medium of the war poster epitomising the modernity of the conflict. War posters constituted a political adaptation of a medium that had already pervaded European cityscapes.

Recruiting posters are often designed to place emotional pressure on people based on longstanding cultural traditions (the family, sentimentalism, military hero, to name a few) by constructing a pictorial rhetoric of national identities, identities on which the waging of war hinged. Without the consent and material support of the Home Front, combatant nations would never be able to sustain the huge losses that a long-term war of attrition entailed.

The Parliamentary Recruiting Committee, or PRC, has provided us with some of the most powerful images of British society during the First World War. The vivid recruiting posters of the campaign have come to be regarded as vital to the mobilisation of popular support for the war, but only one of the designs attributed to it, Alfred Leete's 'Kitchener Wants You' has become an icon of the twentieth century. However, his poster was produced privately by *London Opinion* and, as with others privately produced, does not seem to have reflected the attitudes of government, but rather those of a new breed of commercial advertisers and graphic designers whose involvement in the recruiting campaign was resented by those in power. The rapid growth of a national market for cheap branded goods had brought these advertising experts into prominence, but their rising status inevitably brought them into conflict with the upper and middle classes, whose dominance of consumer retailing they were helping to undermine.

The earliest recruiting posters tended to be blown-up versions of handbills, usually with text in one or two colours, and sometimes simply provided the technical terms of enlistment. Many of the early posters made reference to the German invasion of Belgium in terms of its abrogation of international treaties – the tearing up a 'scrap of paper' – and brutality. Evidence of German attitudes in Belgium is evidenced by the posters they printed during the occupation. Hardie quotes two 1914 posters, held by the IWM: one threatens to kill a third of the male inhabitants should the German troops be fired upon; another states that the authorities had ordered the massacre or burning alive of three hundred people. An example of the latter is the poster 'Remember Scarborough' a reference to that seaside town's bombardment, along with the towns of Hartlepool and Whitby, by German warships on 16 December 1914 (Figure 13). The attack killed 137 people and left almost six hundred wounded, most of them civilians. A graphical version of the poster was produced for the PRC by Lucy Kemp-Welch, an artist renowned for her horse paintings and her book jacket for Anna Sewell's *Black Beauty.*

Over time, the recruitment campaign became more sophisticated and psychologically manipulative. Calls to duty were replaced or supplemented by three elements: appeals to young men's desire for adventure, camaraderie and masculinity ('He's happy and satisfied, are you?' 'There are three types of men' 'What will your pals think of you?'); by demonising Germany and Germans; and by social shaming techniques. Posters that tried to provoke guilt in the general populace were later considered to be especially invidious. The poster 'Daddy, what did you do in the Great War?' by the illustrator Savile Lumley features a middle-aged man in silent repose in his postwar armchair – likely overcome with shame – as his son plays with toy soldiers on the floor (Figure 14). His daughter, resting on his knees and obviously reading an account of the war, asks, in all innocence, the damning question.

The idea has been credited to a printer, Arthur Gunn, who is reported to have imagined himself as the father in question. After seeing a sketch of the scene by Lumley, Gunn joined the Westminster Volunteers.

Guilt was also used in posters that urged women to persuade their men-folk to enlist, by both questioning their men's masculinity and questioning the patriotism of women who hesitated to give up their husbands, fathers and sons to the service of the nation, as in '*Women of Britain, persuade them to go*' (Figure 15).

The war fundamentally changed the way people imagined masculinity and femininity. Initially, war disrupted men's lives by mobilising them into the armed forces, and, in some cases, wounding and killing them. Women's lives, too, changed by their being forced to consider new kinds of labour and at the end of the war they won the vote. But these changes need to be understood in relation to changes in how men and women perceived their own genders – having a male or female body meant something different in 1918 than it had five years earlier. The presence of wounded veterans made it very difficult to ignore how vulnerable male bodies were in an age of industrial war.

Women had been given jobs in labour and literally clothed in new uniforms and consequently viewed their own bodies with a different significance compared with supposedly traditional female roles. Posters were instruments of these changes, linking the concrete world with the imaginary one and conveying information about how men and women could and should contribute to the war. Images of men and women in uniform mixed with old-fashioned ideals worked to forge imaginary alliances between individual bodies and the nation as a whole. Posters provided a new visual vocabulary for picturing men and women in relation to each other, the nation and machines.

The academic Meg Albrinck has emphasised the importance of 'masculinity' in British recruitment posters and how this depiction evolved. As an example, it was strongly suggested that an un-enlisted man would suffer social embarrassment and personal guilt if he did not serve. In the same issue of *London Opinion* that carried Leete's Kitchener cover, the illustrator had a half-page cartoon showing a newly enlisted soldier with a girl on each arm, while a gad-about young man can only look on jealously. It may be considered that British poster makers projected an ideal masculine behaviour, attempting, and maybe succeeding, in manipulating popular attitudes of masculine duty.

Such ideas point up the change in attitudes to war recruitment today. The rich trove of images in World War I posters raises a puzzling question – why, in the Second World War, were similar images generally absent from poster art or indeed from broader imaginings of war? Although the US reused recruiting images for the later conflict, the British authorities did not. It has been suggested that poster images help us see aspects of disenchantment with the twentieth century – a progressive retreat from these representations of war and warriors into more complex and compromised images. Consider also what images of Auschwitz and Hiroshima did to representations of war, and the work of photojournalists such as Don McCullin in magazines and Sunday newspaper supplements in the 1960s. What association was WikiLeaks founder Julian Assange trying to spark in the minds of viewers when he held a 2010 press conference with a massive blow-up of '*Shell-Shocked Marine*', a 1968 Vietnam war photograph by McCullin, behind him?

Recent generations are left with a shifting landscape of imaginings of war: some heroic, others negative, troubled, unresolved, unsettled. The moral conundrum of how to imagine war without glorifying it is with us still. Recruitment into the armed services today is based on images of travel, camaraderie, peace-keeping and skill achievements rather than the 'bullying techniques' and sentimentality of World War I.

Timeline for Leete's image

1882
28 August. Alfred Leete born in Northampton
1885
Kitchener shown on a postcard of a photograph by Alexander Bassano
1897
Leete's first published drawing in the *Daily Graphic*
1905
22 November. Leete's first cartoon for *Punch* published

1906
Advertisement for BDV cigarettes
1912
17 January. Scott and four others reach the South Pole but die on the return journey

1914
15 January. Caxton recruitment advertising starts in national papers
1914
4 August. Britain declares war on Germany
1914
5August. First wartime recruiting advert: Eric Field's 'Your King and Country need you'
1914
7 August. Kitchener's appeal for 100,000 men
1914
2 September. *Punch* magazine prints cartoon poster

1914
5 September. *London Opinion*'s 'Your Country Needs YOU' cover by Leete

1914
14 November. Leete skit on his own *London Opinion* cover

1914
Parliamentary Recruiting Committee starts to issue text posters

1914
PRC's first poster using an image of the British Isles

1914
An army recruiting office covered in posters

1914
November. PRC poster 'Britain's new million army'

1914
Leete began to publish his Schmidt the Spy drawings in *London Opinion*

1915
July. PRC produces the 'official' Kitchener poster

1915
One of several 'Remember Belgium' posters by the PRC

1915
PRC poster uses the Leete image

1915
Cigarette cards of the PRC's posters. Leete's image is not used

1916
March. Conscription comes into force under Military Service Act for unmarried men aged 18-41
1916
Leete's *Schmidt the Spy* made into a film

1916
Leete joins the Artists Rifles. Sees action in France in 1917 and 1918
1916
June. Kitchener lost at sea

1916
6 July. *Leslie's Weekly* magazine carries a US version of Leete's cover by James Montgomery Flagg

1916
13 July. Flagg's Uncle Sam is used for advertising in *Leslie's*

1917
15 February. *Leslie's* again uses Flagg's Uncle Sam with the words, 'I Want You'
1917
5 March. War cabinet approves the creation of a national war museum. Later becomes the Imperial War Museum
1917
6 April. US enters war
1917
19 April. Flagg joins volunteers on US pictorial publicity committee
1917
Flagg's Uncle Sam used for a US army recruiting poster

1917
29 December. A variant of Flagg's image for *Leslie's* with an armed Uncle Sam

1917-20
Leete's concept used the USSR, Germany, Italy and other nations

1918
11 November. War ends with armistice
1918
Leete's 'Masbadges' in the *Sketch* of animal mascots combined with regimental badges
1920
9 June. Imperial War Museum opened in the Crystal Palace by George V
1921-22
Lord Esher biography of Kitchener. Asquith, former prime minister, defends Kitchener

1933

17 June. Leete dies in London, aged 51

1936

Leete's book, the *Work of a Pictorial Comedian* published

1936

7 July. The Duke of York, later George VI, opens Imperial War Museum on present site in South London

1939

3 September. Britain declares war on Germany

1940

June. *Picture Post* uses Leete's artwork in the week of the Dunkirk rescue

1949

George Orwell's *Nineteen Eighty-Four* published

1955

19 March *Picturegoer* magazine uses a Leete-style image to promote its Vote for Your Stars competition

1955

Daily Telegraph magazine uses Leete artwork as one of eight iconic images of the past century

1958

Philip Magnus biography of Kitchener

1961

July 14. *Daily Mail* ridicules Harold Macmillan, the prime minister, as Kitchener

1962

Jump Up records releases Lord Kitchener's 'Love in the Cemetery' single by the Jamaican reggae/calypso band

1964

I was Lord Kitchener's Valet uses posters and shop sign based on Leete's image

1960s

Leete's Kitchener and Flagg's Uncle Sam become icons of youth culture

1997

1 May. *Daily Mirror* front page of Tony Blair on the day he became prime minister

1999

15 October. PRC's Caxton/Leete/Field poster voted second best poster of the century

2002

17 December. PRC's Caxton/Leete/Field poster named best recruitment advert

2003

TV documentary draws on Field's diaries to describe him writing the slogan 'Your country needs you'

2008

September. Economist cover of US Treasury secretary Henry Paulson based on Flagg artwork

2010

6 October. David Cameron invokes Leete's words in a speech on his 'Big Society' theme

2010

9 October. *Sunday Times* montage parodies Cameron's Big Society speech

2011

4 January. *Times* archive website uses Leete's image in its launch material

2013

February. Military History joins the many magazines that have reproduced Leete's image

The popular cartoonist

The advent of *Punch* in 1841 sparked a booming market for cartoonists in Britain. Indeed, the term 'cartoon' in its modern-day sense of a humorous drawing was coined by the humorous weekly in 1843. Before then, a cartoon was a preparatory sketch for an oil painting of the same size, or for a tapestry, mosaic or stained glass window. In the next sixty years, dozens of other titles were launched, many of them with illustration and cartoons at their core. *Cornhill, Illustrated London News*, the *Strand, John Bull, Vanity Fair*, the *Graphic,* the *Sketch, Tatler, Bystander* and their like helped establish and sustain the careers of many artists and illustrators. Photography was in its infancy and it was not until the advent of the half-tone process in the mid-1880s that magazines were able to start experimenting with printing photographs.

The Pre-Raphaelites not only earned their livings from serving the needs of magazines such as *Cornhill,* but even set out their agenda as artists and poets by launching their own magazine, the *Germ* in 1850. *Punch*, meanwhile, had established an unrivalled roster of artists on its staff, such as John Leech, Richard Doyle, John Tenniel and Charles Keene.

It was Tenniel who drew the political cartoon 'Dropping the Pilot' in 1890 that is mimicked to this day and sums up a pivotal event in European politics. The German emperor Wilhelm II watches from the deck as chancellor Otto von Bismarck walks down a staircase at the side of the ship – Bismarck, who was seen as having helped preserve peace in Europe, had been forced to resign after a difference in political views. A cartoon in *Bystander* echoed this image a month after the outbreak of war, showing Bismark striding through water to reach Wilhelm, whose boat has foundered on rocks (Figure 16).

Some Victorian and Edwardian illustrators are still household names – W. Heath Robinson with his world of unlikely machines and the fairies of Arthur Rackham, for example, and the images of many others are familiar even if their names have lost their renown. Supporting them were private art schools, many of them founded by illustrators, such as that of John *'Skegness is So Bracing'* Hassall.

Other famed illustrators who live on with us today include Sidney Paget, whose depictions of Arthur Conan Doyle's Sherlock Holmes in the Strand define the character to this day. The name of Kate Greenaway, a Victorian illustrator, is on an annual medal for the best children's books. Her work, which appeared in many magazines, including *Illustrated London News* covers, was not only popular among readers but also changed the way the Victorians dressed their children. The cute toddlers of Mabel Lucie Attwell's pictures in magazines, from the classy *Tatler* to a cheap women's weekly such as Home Notes were the basis of a range of pottery that was still being made into the 1960s. Attwell also produced a cartoon strip called 'Wot a Life' for *London Opinion* during the second war.

It was only in the final quarter of the twentieth century that it became fast and cheap to reproduce colour photographs in print. Furthermore, until then, the print quality of letterpress halftones – the main printing technique for newspapers and topical magazines – was poor, so it was easier to portray events using sketches. Because of this, some of the most popular illustrators gained superstar status and readers knew them by name. This was certainly the case at the time of the Great War and although photography gained in popularity, the drawn image was still widespread in WWII.

The work of Bruce Bairnsfather was inspired by life in the trenches and made him a household name. His best-known character is Old Bill, whose exploits, along with his pals Bert and Alf, were a weekly feature in the *Bystander* from his first submission in 1915 when he was serving with the 1st Royal Warwickshire Regiment (Figure 17). 'I have drawn it,' he wrote 'as well as I can under somewhat difficult circumstances, and, I may say, from first-hand impressions.' Bairnsfather was injured during the Second Battle of Ypres. Back in Blighty, as the troops called home, he developed his humorous series featuring Old Bill, a curmudgeonly veteran soldier with trademark walrus moustache and balaclava. The best remembered of these shows Bill with another trooper in a muddy shell hole with shells whizzing all around. The other trooper is grumbling and Bill advises: 'Well, if you knows of a better 'ole go to it.' The drawings were later collated in a series of eight books entitled *Fragments from France*, which sold over a million copies with editions published in the US, Canada and Australia. The name 'Old Bill' became a nickname for the police, many of whom came into the force after military service and sported large moustaches such as that depicted on the character.

The title *Better 'Ole* was used for a musical and two films based on the strip in both Britain and the US. Bairnsfather went on to write books and plays, and in 1927 directed a film. He appeared on the stage in London and New York, was one of the first celebrities to be recorded talking on film in the US, and then took part in early television broadcasts from Alexandra Palace. He contributed to *Life*, the *New Yorker* and *Judge* in the US as well as British magazines. Old Bill was resurrected in the Second World War, being published in several magazines and becoming a mascot for the US forces in Britain. Bairnsfather introduced Old Bill's son, Young Bill, and a film was made about them, *Old Bill & Son*. An omnibus that had taken troops to the Western Front was decorated in Old Bill livery after the war and is a feature of the Imperial War Museum in London.

Another cartoonist who fought in the war was Cyril Bird, who was injured at the Battle of Gallipoli. He adopted the pen name Fougasse, after a type of land mine, and began contributing to *Punch* in 1916, with the cartoon 'War's brutalising influence' (Figure 18), as well as the *Graphic* and *Tatler*. He became art editor of *Punch* from 1937 to 1949, then editor until 1953. During World War II he designed many government posters, including the 'Careless Talk Costs Lives' series. In 2009, British Airways began using one of his cartoons for its first class menus, continuing an association that goes back to the 1930s, when Fougasse penned advertising posters for BA's forerunner, Imperial Airways.

William Barribal was already an accomplished painter and designer at the turn of the twentieth century who used his wife as his principal model to create images of exquisite and fashionable Edwardian women. He drew several First World War recruitment posters and worked for various magazines, including *Vogue* and *Pearson's*, as well as producing railway posters and playing cards, these works being keenly sought after today.

Another veteran illustrator was Bert Thomas who worked as a freelance for the *Strand, Pick-Me-Up* and Ally Sloper's *Half Holiday* and in 1905 began an association with *Punch* that led to the magazine publishing more than a thousand of his cartoons. From 1909 he also supplied *London Opinion* with political and social cartoons. However, his most famous offering was produced in the early months of the First World War, when he drew – supposedly in ten minutes – a grinning Tommy lighting a pipe with the caption 'Arf a Mo', Kaiser!' which was published in the *Weekly Dispatch* in 1914 and helped raise £250,000 to send tobacco to the troops. In 1916, Thomas enlisted in the Artists Rifles and served as a war artist for the National Savings campaign. In 1918, he drew the largest poster for an appeal to invest in War Bonds – it covered the facade of the National Gallery in London's Trafalgar Square. Painted in oils, it was seventy-five feet long and showed Drake facing the Spanish Armada. Thomas produced similar posters in Cardiff and Glasgow, and in 1918 was awarded an MBE for his contributions to the war effort. Many of his wartime cartoons, along with those of Wilton Williams, were published as a book by *London Opinion* after the war.

George Studdy contributed to many magazines around the turn of the century, with much of his work based on the portrayal of anthropomorphised animals. In 1921, he invented Bonzo dog for the Sketch. The puppy appeared in many compilation books and advertisements, selling everything from tobacco, cars, soap and polish to confectionery and pickles. He was also used for one of the first neon signs put up in London's Piccadilly Circus. Forty years later, the name inspired Vivian Stanshall's eccentric Bonzo Dog Doo-Dah Band.

Animals also made the name of Lawson Wood, who was employed by Arthur Pearson from 1896 and went on to gain popular acclaim for his depictions of stone-age humans and dinosaurs. The art instructor Percy V. Bradshaw employed him to work on the Art of the Illustrator, a collection of twenty portfolios demonstrating six stages of a single painting or drawing by twenty artists. During World War I, Wood served in the Kite Balloon Wing of the Royal Flying Corps. His work spotting planes from a hot-air balloon led to Wood being decorated by the French.

After the war, his animal designs were reproduced as wooden toys known as the Lawson Woodies. His orangutan character, Gran'pop, ran in the Sketch in the 1930s and featured in animated cinema cartoons in 1940.

Many illustrators were members of the London Sketch Club, which traces its history back to a meeting in 1823 and the formation of the Artists Society in 1830, whose members included *Punch* artists Sir John Tenniel and Charles Keene and book illustrator Arthur Rackham. The London Sketch Club has noted that 1914 saw the 'collapse of the illustrated book market' and that 1939 led to the 'collapse of the illustrated magazine market' in favour of photography.

In the middle of the nineteenth century, Britain came under threat of invasion from the French under Napoleon III. In response, many people volunteered for military service and in 1859 a group of painters, sculptors, engravers, musicians, architects and actors formed the 38th Middlesex (Artists) Rifle Volunteers. Its first commanding officers included the painter Henry Wyndham Phillips and Fredrick Leighton, later president of the Royal Academy. Many of the Pre-Raphaelites signed up for the Artists Rifles, including John Everett Millais, Holman Hunt and William Morris. *Punch* cartoonist John Leech was another member. The regiment served in both the Boer wars and the Great War, with recruits such as sculptor Charles Jagger, Bert 'Arf a Mo' Kaiser' Thomas, the poet Edward Thomas, Harold Earnshaw (illustrator and husband of Mabel Lucie Attwell), and the painters Paul Nash and John Nash. Eight members of the regiment were awarded the Victoria Cross during the Great War. It became a training unit for officers in the Second World War and later was used as the basis for the Special Air Services (SAS).

It was in this tradition that Alfred Leete worked.

Figure 18. Cyril Bird adopted the pen name Fougasse, after a type of land mine. This was his first *Punch* cartoon

Figure 19. Leete in civilian clothes with colleagues from the Artists Rifles

Figure 20. How Leete portrayed a dachshund-led German fleet for *Bystander*

Figure 21. Leete's 'Sanctuary, or the Ever Open Door' (1917)

Alfred Leete, artist and soldier

Alfred Leete was the son of a farmer and born in Northampton on 28 August 1882. The family moved to Weston-super-Mare and he left school at the age of twelve to be an office boy for a surveyor in Bristol. This was followed by jobs as a draughtsman in a furniture company and as a lithographer. At the age of 16, Leete had his first cartoon accepted by the *Daily Graphic*. In 1905, *Punch* accepted one of his drawings. He then became a full-time illustrator and as well as drawing cartoons, found success designing posters and as a commercial artist. His drawings appeared in many magazines, including the *Pall Mall Gazette*, the *Bystander*, *London Opinion* and the *Sketch*.

Leete drew the Lord Kitchener 'Your country needs you' image for the 5 September 1914 cover of the weekly magazine *London Opinion*. The previous month, he had designed a frontispiece, 'Get out and get under', for the *Bystander* showing the German fleet cowering in a kennel with a dachshund because the Royal Navy, with a bulldog, is approaching on the horizon (Figure 20). (The veteran *Punch* cartoonist Lewis Baumer also portrayed a dachshund as a 'social pariah' and it was used to represent Germany by other cartoonists.) Leete provided the illustrations for several books including *All the Rumours* and the *Bosch Book* in 1916. His popular '*Schmidt the Spy*' strip for *London Opinion* drew on the 'spy fever' at the time, not only in Britain, where Carl Hans Lody, a German naval reservist was shot in the Tower of London as a spy on 5 November 1914, but also in France and Germany. The character was turned into a silent film in April 1916 with Lewis Sydney playing Schmidt, an inept German infiltrator. The spy mania continued, notes Michael MacDonagh in his diaries, but by the end of 1916 he describes it as generating 'nosey parkers' who are a source of nuisance, but an amusement to most people.

Leete joined the Artists Rifles in 1916 and was sent to France in 1917 and 1918 (Figure 20).

As well as Leete's Kitchener image being used as a war poster, he later designed recruitment posters for the tanks corps with headlines such as 'Become a Motor Engineer and See the World!', 'See the World – and Get Paid for Doing It' and 'Wanted. Smart Men for the Tank Corps – Let Professor Tank Teach You a Trade'. These themes have continued in use in military recruitment right up to the present day.

After the war, Leete produced a series for the *Sketch* called 'Masbadges', of fantastical creatures made up by combining animal mascots with the badges of their regiment. These included a leek-nosed goat of the Welsh Guards; a surly-looking bulldog with the insignia of the Royal Artillery for its nose; and the Royal Flying Corps Bird, which looks like a penguin, the beak being formed by the wings of the corps' badge.

Leete went on to produce advertising posters for many products, including Bovril, Connolly Leather, Rowntree's Chocolate and the brewer William Younger as well as producing striking posters for the London Underground. His 'Mr York of York, Yorks' character became the star of the first British animated film commercial with synchronised sound, for Rowntree's Chocolate. Leete's Younger's character, Mr William, was one of the advertising icons chosen by Royal Doulton for four limited edition millennium figures; the others being the Robertson's Golly, Sir Kreemy Knut from Sharp's Toffee and 'Peppy', the Fox's Glacier Mints polar bear.

An advertisement for *London Opinion* in the *Daily Mail* of 18 February 1922 described Leete as 'the funniest man in the world'. He provided the covers and illustrations for the Mrs Bindle stories by Herbert Jenkins in *Pearson's*. His Bovril slogans were used as the basis of a national competition in 1928 and published as the Bovril Slogan Cartoon Book. Leete, described in his obituary as a 'black and white artist and cartoonist' died at home in Pembroke Square, London, after a seizure on 17 June 1933. His signature, alongside those of Bert Thomas and John Hassall were still reported by the *Daily Mail* as being a feature of Sandy's Autograph Bar near Piccadilly Circus in 1939.

Some commentators have described Leete solely as an 'illustrator' and not a 'graphic designer', which implies that the design elements of the Kitchener poster might not have been initiated by him. However, it takes only an observation of his paintings and other poster work, particularly those he produced for London Underground, to show the extent of his design, as well as artistic, skills. His paintings from the trenches, as a member of the Artists Rifles, reveal an artist capable of producing fine work, including the 'Sanctuary, or The Ever Open Door' – a haunting painting of Belgian refugees (Figure 21).

Figure 22. Eric Field's full-page cover advert in the *Daily Mail* in January 1914

Figure 23. The first wartime recruiting advert on 5 August 1914

Figure 24. How the August advert appeared in the *Daily Mail* (page 3)

Figure 25. Kitchener insisted on posters and later adverts ending with 'God save the King'

London Opinion magazine

London Opinion was owned by C. Arthur Pearson, a publishing company named after its founder who had established *Pearson's Weekly*, one of the best-selling Victorian magazines, in 1890. This was a great success from the start, and the proceeds enabled Pearson to establish many magazines and in 1900 to launch the *Daily Express*, sparking a commercial battle with the rival *Daily Mail* that would continue through the century. However, Pearson himself had begun to go blind and from about 1910 sold his newspapers and magazines. The *Daily Express* ended up in the hands of Sir Max Aitken, later Lord Beaverbrook, and the magazine interests, including *London Opinion*, went to a rival magazine publishing company, George Newnes. Pearson then devoted his time to promoting scouting, the National Institution for the Blind and the St Dunstan's Home for soldiers blinded in the Great War. He died in 1921 after a fall in the bath.

London Opinion was founded in 1903 and 'conducted' by A. Moreton Mandeville. Four years later, it ran limerick competitions that led to so many entries that questions were asked in parliament about the great demand for postal orders to pay for the entries. The magazine also sponsored the *Laughter Show*, an international exhibition of humorous art, at Holland Park Hall (11 May to 6 June 1914). Circulation figures are difficult to establish with any certainty at this time, but it was probably selling a quarter of a million copies a week. *London Opinion* continued as a weekly until the November 1939 issue at the outbreak of WWII, when it cut its page size, adopted more colour and went monthly, mimicking the format of *Men Only*, which had been launched in 1935 as a general interest monthly for men. Although the November issue makes reference to the magazine's role in supporting the troops in the Great War, no mention is made of the Leete cover or poster.

London Opinion was the first national title to recognise the talent of twenty-year-old *Cambridge Evening News* cartoonist Ronald Searle by publishing one of his cartoons in 1940, and for the comics historian Denis Gifford, it 'was probably the funniest magazine of its era'. Norman Thelwell, today best known for his cartoons of girls and their dimwitted ponies, also had his first break on *London Opinion*, as did Billy Liar creator and *Daily Mirror* columnist Keith Waterhouse. It was one of the magazines considered to have such popular appeal that it was distributed as recreational reading matter to the fleet during the war. However, *London Opinion* was ultimately owned by the same company as *Men Only*, and was folded into that title in 1954 as the market for general interest men's magazines contracted.

Figure 26. Cartoonists saw censorship as damping the recruitment effort

Figure 27. A selection of the many posters printed during the war

Figure 28. The king reviewing the new army. Note Kitchener's height

Figure 29. 'Arf a mo' Kaiser' by Bert Thomas

The government's recruiting campaign

At the start of the war, many people expected it to be over by Christmas but Lord Kitchener, the newly appointed secretary of state for war, was not convinced. He planned for a long campaign and wanted to raise an army of volunteers. On 6 August 1914, parliament agreed an increase in army strength of half a million men and initiated the Parliamentary Recruiting Committee (PRC). This body was to oversee all official recruitment to meet the targets. The first task in raising 'Kitchener's army' was to call for 100,000 volunteers, aged between nineteen and thirty, at least five foot three inches tall (1.6 metres) and with a chest size greater than 34 inches (86cm). The PRC started its poster campaign, but the ground was already laid with advertising.

In his book *Advertising*, Eric Field relates how the idea of the government advertising for recruits dated back to a discussion during a game of golf on a Wednesday in October 1913. Playing that day were Colonel John Seeley, secretary of state for war; Hedley Le Bas, who had founded Caxton Publishing Company in 1899 and ran a small advertising arm to promote his books; and Sir George Riddell, proprietor of the *News of the World* and a director of Caxton.

The discussion resulted in a ground-breaking £6,000 budget to produce 'real advertising instead of the stilted [classified] advertisements which the government had used for a hundred years or more'. The campaign ran over the winter and used whole pages in the popular dailies, including a *Daily Mail* front page at £350. That whole front page, headed 'What the Army offers', is described by Field as 'the first real advertisement ever used by the government' when it appeared on 15 January (Figure 22).

The campaign was judged a success, with an accompanying booklet exhausting its 50,000 print run within a week and resulting in an extra 4,000 men signing up. So, the War Office authorised another campaign for the autumn and winter of 1914 and expanded the budget to £20,000. Of course, that plan was never carried out. For, in July 1914, a call came through to Field from Colonel Richard Strachey, the assistant adjutant general for recruiting, who 'swore me to secrecy, told me that war was imminent and that the moment it broke out we should have to start advertising at once'.

Field drafted an initial advert headed: 'Your King and Country need you' below the royal coat of arms (Figure 23). It first appeared in newspapers on 5 August, at a size eight inches deep across two of the seven columns at the top of page three (Figure 24). It sought men aged between eighteen and thirty.

Adverts that ran a week later had changed the terms to 'a period of three years or until the war is concluded. Age of enlistment between nineteen and thirty.' The copy ended with 'God save the King' at

Kitchener's insistence, as did many of the early posters (Figure 25). None of these press advertisements was illustrated, apart from the royal crest, and they were managed separately from the PRC poster campaigns.

Twenty-four days after the initial call to arms in the newspapers, the government ran a new advertisement in the press, again with the royal crest. This time, the headline words were 'Your King and Country need you' and the following text of 'Another 100,000 men wanted'. Later adverts switched the message, with the *Daily Mail* of 7 April 1915 showing a map of Britain with the headline 'If the German Army were in Cardiff' and pointing out that Ostend was as near to London as the Welsh capital. It ended with the slogan, 'Your Country Needs You Now.' In 1917, adverts appealed for 'men who understand horses'. For his work on the campaign, Le Bas was appointed to run the government's advertising propaganda and was knighted for his work in 1916.

To mark Trafalgar Day (October 21), a hoarding was erected around the base of Nelson's Column in Trafalgar Square. The *Daily Mail* reported record crowds for the annual celebration with 'many French and Belgian people in the throng'. Of course, the Battle of Trafalgar in 1805 was against the gallant foes of the French fleet, whereas now Britain was going to war to defend France. A wreath laid at the base of the pillar in tribute to the French sailors who fell more than a century earlier described them as 'compatriots of our comrades in arms today'. Marie de Pereot wrote a letter to the *Daily Mail*:

'Never in history has an allied country been more lavish with its resources and men than is Great Britain at the present moment; her heroic sons are shedding their blood for my country; my people welcome "Tommy" as a brother.'

Pictures in the French weekly *L'Illustration* show crowds milling around a massive poster with a royal crest on either side of King George V's morale-boosting words: 'We are fighting for a worthy purpose and we shall not lay down our arms until that purpose has been achieved.' Another side of the hoarding quoted the famous naval signal hoisted by Nelson at the start of the battle: 'England expects that every man this day will do his duty.'

The *Times* journalist Michael MacDonagh recalls seeing his first recruiting poster on August 6 and cites several examples in his diaries, which were published twenty years later. In the entry for 3 January 1915, he describes London in wartime, with the streets still thronged, but the clocks stopped and church bells silenced:

'Posters appealing for recruits are to be seen on every hoarding, in most shop windows, on omnibuses, tramcars and commercial vans. The great base of the Nelson Pillar is covered with them. Their number and variety are remarkable. Everywhere Lord Kitchener sternly points a monstrously big finger, exclaiming "I Want You".'

Many commentators may have conflated the most memorable image (Leete's portrayal of Kitchener) with the most memorable words ('Your country needs you'). Also, in many places, the posters were probably juxtaposed or pasted on top of each other.

The editorial in most newspapers and magazines reinforced the patriotic image of the man in uniform portrayed in government posters and advertising. Peace protests were reported but usually in negative terms and those avoiding signing up were the butt of jokes in both words and cartoons. However, the press was soon complaining through both articles and cartoons about heavy-handed censorship by the government and blamed this for hindering recruitment because there was no news to report. A *Bystander* cartoon, 'What damps recruiting ardour' shows the censor as a grumpy old woman pouring water over potential recruits from a balcony above the entrance to a recruiting office (Figure 26). The caption quotes the novelist and journalist Arnold Bennett writing in the Daily News about the paucity of information available to the press: 'The British War Office gave [only] eight lines in seven days concerning the deeds of what is admittedly one of the very finest armies known to modern history. And then it is alarmed because recruiting has fallen off.'

William Allen in his book on the history of the printing firm David Allen & Sons, which printed many of the PRC's posters from its plant in Harrow, north London, states that the government's poster campaign was sparked by a recruiting poster of September 1914 for the London Underground by Frank Brangwyn. The idea caught on slowly, with small, letterpress exhortations, but blossomed in 1915 when the pictorial poster came into its own. He quotes the *Billposter* magazine:

> 'Such an illustration of poster power has been given as no country and no age ever saw before.'

Sherlock Holmes creator Sir Arthur Conan Doyle was so impressed he urged the use of posters for a nationwide temperance campaign. By 15 April, three million posters had been issued at a cost of £7,750. But after this bonanza, life became difficult for billposters in 1915.

The main reason was the shortage of materials. Supplies of Swedish pulp for paper-making began to fall off because of a lack of British coal exports. The Swedish mills produced mechanical pulp – made from crushing trees – and chemical pulp, made from boiling trees, hence the need for coal to boil the wood. The latter process produced the much better paper, which was used for posters and the better magazines and books. Newsprint, on the other hand, was 75 per cent mechanical pulp and the rest chemical – that is why is goes brown and falls apart so quickly. Also, artificial inks made from coal-tar dyes produced in Germany were no longer available so lithographers had no artificial blues and reds. They had to go back to using inorganic dyes such as vermilion, chrome, umber, ochre, ultramarine and bronze-blue, and the price of these multiplied.

Then, the government's poster campaign slackened off and in 1916, the advent of conscription saw a shortage of billposters.

Women soon took their place, although 'they needed courage, especially the first pioneers, to face the male ribaldry to which the public nature of their work inevitable exposed them' when pasting up bills made up of up to thirty-two sheets – about ten feet by thirteen feet – from a ladder. In 1917, the maximum size of posters was reduced under paper restriction orders and imports reduced to half the total of the previous year. The government took over the Harrow factory of David Allen & Co.

The PRC's poster campaign was enormous. According to its records, the main recruiting drive involved producing more than 140 poster designs, from which no fewer than 5.7 million full-sized posters were printed plus half a million smaller strip posters for use on taxi cabs, trams and railway carriages (Figure 27). Most of the PRC designs were issued in single sheet, double crown size (30 by 20 inches) rather than the larger eight-sheet (80 by 60 inches), sixteen or thirty-two sheet size favoured by commercial advertisers. This campaign ran for little more than a year generating an average of three new designs a week. It was much larger than any previous publicity campaign run by the government. A search on the web for WWI recruiting posters will indicate the thousands that were printed during the war. The PRC's poster campaign was not designed to create enthusiasm for the war but to sustain it. Kitchener asked for 100,000 recruits and within weeks almost 300,000 men had come forward in an unprecedented show of patriotism.

The *Daily Telegraph's* centenary magazine stated that Kitchener had written to the lords lieutenant of counties and the chairmen of the Territorial Force Associations on August 10 seeking their support. The next day, the weekly average of 500 recruits coming forward had jumped sharply: 'Now the number to enlist daily is as much as 3,000.' The September 30 issue of *Bystander* ran photographs of the king reviewing 'Kitchener's own' at Aldershot (Figure 28). That month, the prime minister said that 'recruiting is going on so fast ... whether we should not dampen it down'. In October, the PRC was asked to restore the previous level of enlistment.

The first poster that the PRC designed carried only text: 'England Expects Every Man to do His Duty'. The first pictorial poster was PRC11 in late October 1914 when more than one million men had already volunteered. The PRC continued to issue pictorial posters until September 1915 by which time the trend of recruiting was steadily downwards. Later, based on evidence gained from recruits, the authorities decided that the most effective designs were not those that bullied potential recruits but rather those that projected 'a delightful geniality'. A good example was the late 1915 poster showing a soldier stopping to light a pipe remarking 'Arf a mo' Kaiser' painted by Bert Thomas (Figure 29).

Figure 30. 'Remember Belgium'

Figure 31. Leete's 'None but the brave' in *London Opinion* suggested the attraction of a man in uniform

Figure 32 'To the Women of Britain ... Send a Man To Join The Army Today'

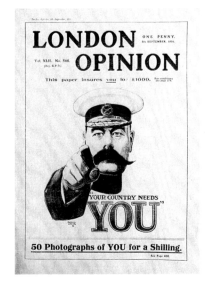

Figure 33. Front cover of *London Opinion*, 5 September 1914

The British advertising industry had a long-term goal of controlling full-scale political campaigns. Advertising experts were confident that they could teach the public about politics 'in the same way they taught them about Coleman's mustard'.

Industry experts suggested similar tactics to central government and in 1913 the War Office was urged to adopt 'modern' methods to sell the idea of joining the ranks of the army.

Before the PRC, British advertisers had made an effort to modernise the political process, but they encountered resistance from those who believed that modern advertising had no part to play in the democratic process – there is good evidence that the so-called 'brash commercialism' of advertising was anathema to both politicians and civil servants.

By April 1915, official recruiting posters were largely indistinguishable from contemporary advertisements and poster designers freely mixed the official imagery with the consumer advertising they continued to produce. A politician is reported as stating that 'a method which might have been unexceptional for calling attention to the virtues of a shop, a soap, a circus or a pill, seemed inappropriate in the case of a great nation struggling at the crisis of its fate'. By June 1915, public resentment started to creep in, and the campaign was described as 'bullying by poster'. 'Daddy, what did you do in the Great War' was overwritten by 'I tried to stop the bloody thing my child!'. Commercialism inevitably started to creep in as in 1915 when the PRC even converted a tobacco advertisement into a poster (PRC 63) with the acknowledgment 'Reproduced by kind permission of Messrs. Abdulla & Co. Ltd.'

One theme was repeated many times, the 'Remember Belgium' poster issued initially by the PRC in November 1914 as PRC 16 (Figure 30). In the centre of the poster stands a fighting man in khaki, his rifle resting on the ground, his eyes looking towards the viewer. Behind him to the left, a fire destroys a village and sends black smoke billowing across the sky. To the right, a woman flees with an infant and a toddler. While she looks back over her shoulder, the toddler looks forward and reaches a small hand towards the man in khaki. At the bottom of the poster appears the command 'Enlist To-day.'

This poster invites the viewer to consider the alleged immorality of the German armies and to take up arms against them. Two structural devices are employed to imply that enlistment is a moral option for defeating barbarity. First, fighting is depicted as a humanitarian act – as helping women and children – so disguising the brutality in which the soldier will have to participate. Framing battle in this way, the image depicts the government's appeal through the outstretched hand of the child, covering national interests with personal ones. Second, the positioning of the soldier, standing between the fire and the fleeing family, suggests that enlistment will directly protect women and children. Just as the soldier in the poster stands between the family and the fire raging behind them, so the viewer will be able to stand between other innocents and German barbarism. Some 140,000 copies of this poster were distributed. The PRC avoided more explicit reference to the many atrocity stories, choosing against depicting scenes of a gruesome character and focusing in a more uplifting way on the character of the men who served. However, the public will have been well aware of German 'atrocities' from the press.

For example, the October 1915 execution of 49-year-old British nurse Edith Cavell was portrayed in a *London Opinion* cartoon, 'Britons. Avenge!' with a bugler standing over the prone body of the nurse and sounding a call. The caption ran: 'The brutal murder of Nurse Cavell by the Germans sent a thrill of horror through the civilised world.' Cavell was matron of a training school for nurses in Brussels and stayed on after the city fell in the first few weeks of the war. She cared for wounded soldiers irrespective of nationality and was arrested after helping Allied soldiers escape to Holland. Cavell admitted to the charges and was sentenced to death. Diplomatic efforts to persuade the authorities to commute the sentence were rejected and she was executed by firing squad. As well as journalists running the story, a propaganda campaign publicised the incident and the Essex recruitment committee produced a poster of a photograph of Cavell with the text: 'Murdered by the Huns. Enlist in the 99th and help stop such atrocities.' Cavell herself was reported as saying as she awaited her fate: 'Patriotism is not enough. I must have no hatred or bitterness for anyone.' She was hailed as a heroine and martyr with a statue just off Trafalgar Square and the Cavell Nurses' Trust that helps nurses in time of need was set up in her name in 1917.

The PRC hardened its campaign by threatening un-enlisted man with public reproach. This followed a trend already seen in the magazines. In the very issue of *London Opinion* that first carried Leete's Kitchener image, the artist portrayed a man in uniform with a woman on each arm while a wimp in the background looks on (Figure 31).

Many other illustrators produced cartoons that ridiculed men who did not sign up. And pressure was applied across society. Such was the demand to conform that the War Comments column in *Bystander* referred to readers' letters criticising the fact that the man shown on the cover of the magazine was not in uniform (16 September). The next week, the title was replaced by two soldiers scanning the horizon from a fortified gun emplacement. The magazine also dubbed itself 'the illustrated war review.' The title artwork had already been changed from the peacetime version showing a seated man reading *Bystander* and bracketed by two women, to the man and women looking out with binoculars over the coast with smoke in the distance. Below, the devil was shown throwing dice (26 August). The covers changed again in 1915, portraying the man back at home with the women, but in uniform with his arm in a sling – a 'Blighty wound' in the jargon of the day

56

So, posters appeared proclaiming 'You're proud of your pals in the Army of course! But what will your pals think of you? – Think it over!' And 'Do you feel happy as you walk along the streets and see other men wearing the King's uniform?', the implication being that a 'real' man would be ashamed to face his peers in anything but khaki. Men who did not enlist were deliberately rejecting a tradition of supportive masculine camaraderie in the army, rejecting the needs of comrades and damaging their masculinity. A 1915 recruiting poster by Frank Brangwyn makes it clear: 'Your friends need you – Be a man.' A direct implication is that refusing to volunteer rendered you neither a good friend, nor a man. Words such as 'Why are you stopping here when your pals are out there?' and 'Think! Are you content for him to fight for you? Won't you do your bit?' were blunt statements, as were: 'Come into the ranks and fight for your King and Country – Don't stay in the crowd and stare' and 'It is far better to face the bullets than to be killed at home by a bomb.' These posters used few colours, emphasising the text only and carry a message that would have been more powerful in 1914 than today. By June 1915 the PRC was abrupt in its approach, declaring: 'There are three types of men: Those who hear the call and obey, those who delay, and – the others. To which do you belong?'

For all the volume and variety of posters, the mediocrity of most designs when judged on artistic merit alone has been commented on. In his 1921 book, *War Posters*, Martin Hardie reviewed the best examples on both sides and noted that the IWM had collected twenty thousand examples and the V&A several hundred from all nations. The book focuses on artistic merit and condemns most of the British effort: 'The earliest days of the war saw available spaces everywhere covered with posters cheap in sentiment, and conveying childish and vulgar appeals to a patriotism already stirred far beyond the conception of the artists who designed them or the authorities responsible for their distribution.'

For Hardie:

'We had much to learn from the concentrated power, the force of design, the economy of means, which made German posters sing out from a wall like a defiant blare of trumpets ··· the posters of Germany have a force and character that make most of our own seem insipid and tame.'

In particular, the PRC 'possessed poor degree of artistic perception, and, added to this, a very low notion of the mentality of the British public'. He does go on to admit that the PRC efforts improved in 1915, with examples from Bernard Partridge, Guy Lipscombe, Doris Hatt, Walter Caffyn and Leonard Ravenhill. He has a special mention for Gerald Spencer Pryse, who was in Belgium when war broke out and saw the fighting and the refugees before he was himself injured. As a dispatch-rider, he carried lithographic stones with him and made his drawings directly on them, not on paper. The outstanding figure for Hardie, both in quantity and technical accomplishment, was Frank Brangwyn. However, he notes that:

> 'Among the best and most efficient [posters] may be mentioned Alfred Leete's "Kitchener". But if one compares Leete's head of Kitchener, "Your Country Needs You", with Louis Oppenheim's "Hindenberg", the latter, with its rugged force and reserve of colour, stands as an example of the direction in which Germany tends to beat us in poster art.'

There is no mention of *London Opinion*, or of the likelihood that Leete's image was produced in less than an afternoon. This suggests that Hardie, probably the country's foremost expert on poster art, was unaware that Leete's image had been knocked off at short notice for a magazine cover.

Maurice Rickards, the graphic designer and ephemera encyclopaedist, puts the blame for poor quality at the door of civil servants commissioning printers to do the work: 'result was a remorseless flow of pernickety coloured drawings from printers' "art departments".' He quotes the printer Arthur Gunn claiming the ideas for forty-three designs: 'I used to conceive an idea for recruiting, get a sketch made myself by our own artist ⋯ and take it round to No. 11 Downing Street. If they liked it, no one else could stop it.'

Although Rickards champions the artistry of Brangwyn and Pryse (who were commissioned by Frank Pick for the London Underground), 'Daddy, what did you do in the Great War' is probably more widely remembered.

By April 1915, the Stationery Office had printed more than three million posters and officials were adding to this total at the rate of 600,000 a month – six posters were needed to bring one recruit! This created tremendous problems logistically and in July the publications department suspended its production with a million posters remaining in store. Many tonnes of these were then sent overseas and by the end of September, with declining recruitment, the pictorial poster campaign was suspended.

Figure 34. Poster produced by *London Opinion* in 1914

Figure 35. Photograph of Kitchener by Alexander Bassano (c1885)

Figure 36. Postcard of the Bassano photograph of Kitchener

Figure 37. Painting of Kitchener by A. Davies (1915)

The experience of Kitchener's recruits

On 7 August 1914 Kitchener made his appeal for 100,000 recruits. One strategy was an appeal to men from the same communities or workplaces. In Liverpool, Lord Derby enlisted the local press to promote the idea of 'pals battalions'. He addressed a packed meeting with the words:

> 'This should be a battalion of pals, a battalion in which friends from the same office will fight shoulder to shoulder for the honour of Britain and the credit of Liverpool.'

Within days, more than a thousand men had been recruited, at such a rate that recruitment was temporarily halted. Many of these men will have been fans of Liverpool football club and stood on the Anfield ground's terrace, which was named after the battle of Spion Kop where the British army had suffered a heavy defeat at the hands of the Boer forces in 1900. As part of the Kings Regiment Liverpool, which dated back to 1685, these Pals would normally have worn as a cap badge the White Horse of Hanover, but George V approved the Eagle and Child badge, the Derby family crest, in recognition of the recruiting campaign. Liverpool formed four battalions, each of a thousand men, many of them workmates from the same district. A shortage of equipment meant training with just one old rifle for every ten men, who were billeted in makeshift camps in local parks and Derby's own estate.

By the end of September, more than fifty towns and cities had formed Pals battalions. Derby's reward was to be appointed director of recruiting. *Punch* marked the success of the appointment a year later in a full-page cartoon by 'Craven Hill' (Leonard Raven-Hill): Derby is shown as a recruiting sergeant at the head of a stream of men coming from hills and factories far and near.

After a year's training, the Liverpool battalions left for France. Seven months later, they faced the slaughter of the Somme and some of the heaviest losses ever suffered by the British army. Almost twenty thousand men were killed in a day and twice as many wounded. The Liverpool Pals took the village of Montauban from the Germans, one of the few successes, but two hundred of them were killed. Days later, the same divisions lost five hundred men – 'Liverpool's blackest day'. Other divisions took even worse losses: of 720 Accrington Pals, 584 were killed, wounded or missing; the Leeds Pals lost 750 out of 900; and other battalions lost half of their men. The Liverpool Pals went on to fight at Arras, Ypres and Passchendaele.

Once conscription was introduced in 1916, no more Pals battalions were recruited and most were amalgamated into other battalions. The Liverpool Pals were sent to train US troops; others went to Russia. In total, almost three thousand Liverpool Pals were killed during the Great War and the campaign in Russia.

Figure 38. Photograph of Kitchener
(1916)

Figure 40. BDV cigarette advert

Figure 39. Leete's drawing compared with Bassano's photograph

The Kitchener posters

Once newspapers such as the *Times* and *Daily Mail* carried Eric Field's advertisement at the outbreak of war with its call to arms, 'Your King and Country need you. Will you answer your country's call?', the message was clear, only the image of Lord Kitchener's face was missing.

From the cover of the 5 September 1914 issue of *London Opinion*, the dramatic face of Kitchener peered above his pointing finger with the words 'Your country needs YOU', an obvious reference to words of the newspaper advertising campaign (Figure 33). This cover image was designed by Alfred Leete and owed little either to the War Office or to the Parliamentary Recruiting Committee. Leete was a professional cartoonist and the approach he used ran counter to the official tradition of recruiting in the name of the king and when the PRC was still only using typographical posters. Kitchener initially refused to have himself used by official recruiters and there is no record that he authorised the use of this image by Leete, who would in any case have been unlikely to even think of seeking permission. The raison d'être of most cartoonists and their magazines was to poke fun at political figures.

The poster, as opposed to the magazine cover, was issued during September and October 1914. It was developed directly from Leete's artwork and carried the words 'BRITONS [Kitchener] wants YOU' and its production was a wholly private venture (Figure 34. This was not the only example of a private recruiting appeal. In its issue of 2 September 1914, *Punch* had its eponymous inspiration portrayed as a recruiting sergeant. James Crossley Eno, the manufacturer of Eno's Fruit Salt, had already purchased a painting by Frank Dadd called 'Follow the Drum' and had transformed that into a recruiting poster.

An even closer parallel came from Lord Northcliffe's *Weekly Despatch,* which in November 1914 had carried a photo-montage of a wounded soldier on the battlefield with an inset of a football crowd and the caption 'Will They Never Come?' Northcliffe's Associated Newspapers reproduced this design as a recruiting poster, and issued it free to cinemas in the form of a lantern slide, leading the War Office to congratulate Northcliffe on 'a brilliant contribution to the recruiting campaign'.

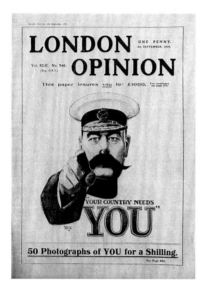

Figure 41. Front cover of *London Opinion*

Figure 42. US Leslie's advert uses James Montgomery Flagg's artwork

Figure 43. Flagg design on a US recruiting poster (1917)

Analysing Leete's poster

When we think of Lord Kitchener the face that comes to mind is the one remembered from the poster; we feel that we know the face. However, the face we visualise is not that of Kitchener at all but of a drawing made by Alfred Leete.

There are some forty-nine photographs of Kitchener in the National Portrait Gallery, many done between 1885 and 1900. Some of these photographs were reprinted as cards, which enjoyed a wide circulation. The most popular and best known card used a photograph taken of him in 1885 by Alexander Bassano, one of the leading portrait photographers of his day, and this was probably the image used by Leete for his artwork (Figure 35).

The Bassano photograph was taken nineteen years before Leete made the drawing and the artist may well have used it, or one of the many thousands of postcards that reproduced it, not only because it portrayed Kitchener as a heroic, handsome man but as the most known image of him at the time (Figure 36). Few portraits exist of Kitchener after 1900, although there is a flattering painting of him from 1915 by A. Davies in Cheltenham Art Gallery (Figure 37).

However, a photograph taken in 1915 shows perhaps more what he would really have looked like at the time, a far older and less healthy person (Figure 38).

Leete took some artistic licence with the image. Kitchener had a divergent 'squint' and Leete removed this divergence, focusing the gaze directly on the viewer.

In addition, he increased the area around the eyes and drew the face slightly longer and more square; the moustache was drawn larger and blacker and forms a massive arrow in the centre of the picture.

Kitchener had a reputation for his 'piercing gaze' but this was perhaps due to his squint and not the image that has remained with us from the face that Leete drew. These staring eyes remove the distinction between Kitchener the poster and Kitchener the general, contributing to the victory of the former over the latter. The general's eyes left a deep impression on his contemporaries: 'Their colour is quite beautiful (a journalist wrote) – as deep and as clear a blue as the sea, in its most azure moments – and they look out at the world, with the perfect directness of a man who sees straight to his end.'

Kitchener's eyes are discussed again, as an epitome of his life and character, in the official three-volume biography published in 1916, shortly after his tragic death in the wreck of the Hampshire: 'Even the eyes, on whose steely qualities so many have dwelt, were not young or brilliant – too much sand had blown in them for that; and there was a slight – a very slight – divergence between them ...' A contemporary journalist indicated the same detail, in a more disparaging tone, while Kitchener was still alive:

> "'About the eyes of Kitchener it may be said without offence that the terror they inspire is heightened by a squint which has tended to grow more pronounced with age ... they would be difficult eyes to face, but with this irregularity they fill certain men with a veritable paralysis of terror." Someone who knows him very well has described to me the effect of those eyes upon people who meet him for the first time: "They strike you," I was told, "with a kind of clutching terror; you look at them, try to say something, look away, and then trying to speak, find your eyes returning to that dreadful gaze, and once more choke with silence."'

For Kitchener's admirers even his slight physical defect, not visible in the posters, became part of his posthumous legend: 'His gaze was somewhat strange, due, no doubt, to a slight divergence of the visual axes – a gaze which no one talking to him could wholly meet, however boldly he might stare. The Sphinx must look like that.'

Yet Leete's pointing finger design is far from an original idea. A 1906 poster for BDV, then a leading brand of cigarettes that was owned by Godfrey Phillips, showed a pointing man whose eyes were in the very centre of the poster and which consequently 'followed the observer everywhere, as did the pointing finger' (Figure 40). W. Macqueen-Pope, an authority on the British stage, wrote about some of the people who worked for David Allen & Co, the poster printers:

> 'There was James Motherwell, a fine, good-looking man from Belfast [whose] face became famous on a nationwide scale. Allens, who did much commercial as well as theatrical work, produced a poster for a famous firm of cigarettes – BDV. It showed a packet of the cigarettes and a very good-looking dark man ⋯ That man was James Motherwell.'

The paragraph goes on to mention that Motherwell was dead. Research in the Commonwealth War Graves Commission records reveals that he was a private in the Dorsetshire Regiment who died aged 41 on 18 November 1917. He is buried at the Baghdad (North Gate) War Cemetery, in what was then Mesopotamia and is now Iraq.

The text on the poster can be regarded as being just as important as the graphic image. The magazine cover had the words 'Your country needs YOU' (the words we remember) and the recruitment poster reads 'BRITONS [Kitchener] wants you' using a very similar type face. Words such as 'needs', 'wants' and 'you' would have had a strong effect on readers at this time and copywriters such as Eric Field used the pronoun 'you' freely in their copy. Similarly, on the front cover of the *London Opinion*, Leete's drawing of Kitchener was accompanied by two messages: 'This paper insures YOU for £1,000' and '50 photographs of YOU for a shilling'.

Figure 44. Some variants by other nations between (1915-19)

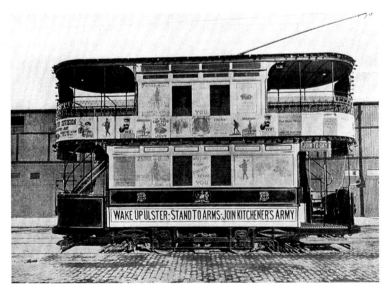

Figure 45. *London Opinion* poster among others on an Ulster tram (1914)

The Kitchener poster copied

Soon after it came out in 1914, Alfred Leete's 'Kitchener' image was copied with good effect by others, initially by other countries to aid their own recruitment or fund-raising efforts but eventually by all sorts of organisations and people promoting ideas, goods and events.

On 6 July 1916, *Leslie's Weekly* ran a James Montgomery Flagg cover for an issue of the US magazine that mimicked Leete's image but with a pointing Uncle Sam. The wording ran: 'What are you doing for preparedness?' Seven days later, Leslie's used Flagg's artwork in an advert. The magazine's publishers were selling a four-volume set called The Great Republic: An illustrated history of the American people (Figure 42).

Beside the image of Flagg's Uncle Sam, the advert's text – playing on the forthcoming presidential election of 1916 – reads:

'Know the facts about your own country. You are soon going to exercise your most important right as a citizen of this great republic by helping to decide who is to be your next president. To make a wise choice of candidates it is important that you should know American facts bearing on the vital questions of the hour.'

The copy goes on to echo the previous week's appearance of Flagg's Uncle Sam by linking to the issue of 'preparedness' by stating:

'Trade conditions have made it possible for us to secure on favourable terms a few sets of these intensely interesting volumes, and as our own contribution toward real PREPAREDNESS at this opportune time we will offer these sets, while they last, to quick buyers at a wonderful bargain.'

Just as Leete had done before, Flagg did a variant of his image for a later edition of *Leslie's* and went on to use it for a recruiting poster (Figure 43).

The Leete poster design was also mimicked by a number of other nations between 1915 and 1919 (Figure 44). A poster of a very similar style was posted outside of the Bank of New Zealand in 1915 and a Canadian recruiting poster of the same year uses the same iconography. Thousands of imitations have followed over the years and most readers will have seen one.

A browse in a web search engine for the words 'Leete Kitchener poster' or '*London Opinion* poster' or 'Kitchener poster' will produce a cacophony of images.

Figure 46. Leete's Kitchener poster outside Chester barracks

Figure 47. Liverpool Exchange Station (National Railway Museum)

Was the Kitchener poster effective?

Much has been written about the effectiveness (or not) of Alfred Leete's Lord Kitchener poster as a recruiting tool but the evidence is anecdotal. In any case, it would be impossible to separate out the effect of one recruitment method from the myriad of efforts to work out with any certainty how many men were persuaded to enlist because of it. The recruitment campaign was certainly regarded as effective. On 16 November, the prime minister gave a statement about the recruitment numbers:

> 'I can give the total number of persons who have been recruited. Roughly – I do not want to commit myself precisely – since the week ending the 10th of August, approximately – I do not say much more, but certainly not less than – 700,000 recruits have joined the Colours, and they are still coming in very steadily. They have nothing to do with the Territorials. We must add to that a very large number of Territorials, at least 200,000, and I think more. I do not think that I should be very far short of the mark if I said that a million men had been recruited since the first appeal was made in the first week in August.'

By Christmas, another 218,000 names of persons willing to serve had been collected from the distribution of householders' forms by the Parliamentary Recruiting Committee to country towns and districts, and the forms were then going out to large towns and cities. Policy changed in the new year, however, with actual numbers no longer being released. Instead, Viscount Midleton told parliament the figures were 'remarkable' and gave percentages of recruits raised per 10,000 of the population, deliberately so the exact figure was obscured.

He raised a concern that the industrial areas were bearing too high a price compared with rural areas. From August 4 to November 4, the southern district of Scotland furnished 237 recruits per 10,000 of the population; Warwickshire and the Midland counties, 196; Lancashire, 178; London and the Home Counties, 170; Yorkshire, Durham and Northumberland, 150; Cheshire and part of Lancashire and the neighbouring Welsh counties, 135; the North of Ireland, including Dublin, Wicklow, Carlow, and Kildare, 127; Notts and Derbyshire, 119; North of Scotland 93; West of England, 88; East of England, 80 per 10,000; and in the South and West of Ireland, 32 per 10,000 of the population. The cost incurred by the PRC was estimated at £10,000. By May, forms to households had produced the names of 300,000 men willing to enlist. By the end of 1915, 2,466,719 had voluntarily enlisted. In total, 5.7 million men served compared with 3.8 million in World War II.

In 1997, an article in the Imperial War Museum Review, '*Kitchener wants you and Daddy what did you do in the Great War? The myth of British recruiting posters*' by Nicholas Hiley, claimed that the poster was not well known during the war but became iconic after the museum acquired Leete's artwork and used the image on its publicity. Hence, it claims credit for the public association of the image with the war. The article points out that the poster was not recorded in the files of the PRC, in the War Office, or the published accounts of the printers, David Allen & Sons, or in the newspapers and magazines which at the time regularly criticised such posters. There is no evidence that Leete's was an official design, for it did not carry a PRC number or a Stationery Office imprint. It is not referred to in PRC minutes, listed in the poster catalogues or included in the official summary of its work. Indeed, the PRC issued its own, officially called 'Kitchener poster', which had wide circulation. This poster, often dated 1914, may well have been printed in 1915 because it quoted from a speech Kitchener gave at the London Guildhall in July 1915 stressing the call of duty.

In an interview with one of the authors in July 2010, Richard Slocombe, senior curator of art at the Imperial War Museum, repeated the view that the poster itself received little exposure during the war years. The effectiveness of Leete's rendition of Kitchener, it claims, has to be measured against the almost complete absence of contemporary references to it, either as the *London Opinion* front cover or as it was later issued by the printers David Allen & Sons with the words 'Britons, [Kitchener] wants YOU'.

It is, however, not difficult to explain the lack of reference to an image regarded as widespread and that left such an impression on so many people: It was not official, therefore, would not have been displayed at recruiting offices, railway stations and other sites that were part of the government's network. It was privately produced in relatively small numbers and its distribution network will have been very different, too. Copies of the poster may well have been sent out with bundles of magazines to be displayed outside newsagents, as much to encourage sales as to recruit troops. As such, many of the posters will have been on display for just a week or even a few days before being replaced by a promotional poster for a different issue or magazine.

In 2013, the book *Your Country Needs You* by James Taylor repeated the Nicholas Hiley argument and cited the lack of evidence both written and photographic. This is misleading as there are authenticated photographs of the Leete poster displayed on a recruiting tram in Ulster (Figure 45) as well as Chester (Figure 46) and Liverpool (Figure 47), together suggesting that the poster was distributed across the country.

Figure 47 is a clear example of the Kitchener poster in situ. It is a photograph showing it with other contemporary posters at Liverpool's Exchange Station. The photograph is part of the Horwich collection, which represents the work of photographers employed by the Lancashire & Yorkshire Railway and its successors, the London & North Western Railway, London Midland & Scottish Railway and British Railways between 1890 and 1979. In 1914, this would have been the Lancashire and Yorkshire Railway, which ran routes through Liverpool. The date of the photograph, 15 December 1914, is taken from the handwritten log of the photographer and the authors have seen the original full-plate glass negative. The poet Siegfried Sassoon frequently lodged in the hotel adjoining Liverpool Exchange Station and it was there in 1917 that he wrote 'A Soldier's Declaration', a watershed in attitudes towards the war that appeared in the press and was read to the House of Commons.

Counter to the argument that the specific words 'Your Country Needs You' were never on a poster is the fact that within a year of the *London Opinion* cover, a poster was produced by David Allen & Sons with Leete's image and the words 'Your Country Needs You' (Figure 49). A copy of this is in the Imperial War Museum.

Immediately after the war, the museum, which was founded in 1917, considered the artwork important enough to obtain it and claims that it was the IWM that promoted the image must be balanced against the lack of records about any of their publicity bearing the Leete image and it was not included in a touring exhibition of war posters organised by the museum in 1917 (although the Leete poster was featured in an exhibition in 1919). So we know that there were at least three posters using the Alfred Leete artwork with various texts. Claiming that a poster with a particular image and a specific text may not have been widely circulated is an exercise in semantics. Claiming that the many references to the poster in veterans' memoirs and interviews are incorrect because of their failing memories is giving the people concerned little credit.

Furthermore, several European countries considered the Leete idea so impressive that they quickly did their own versions. In the US, New York artist James Montgomery Flagg copied Leete's image, first for a cover of Leslie's Weekly magazine, then for advertising and then for a recruitment poster. Four million copies of Flagg's 'I want YOU for the US Army' poster of 1917 were printed (Figure 43). A poster of a similar style was posted outside of the Bank of New Zealand in 1915 (Figure 50) and a Canadian recruiting poster of the same year uses the same iconography (Figure 51). An adaptation of Leete's poster, featuring a bearded man in a turban pointing at the viewer, was used in India with the text 'Have you bought war bonds or not?' in Gujarati towards the end of the war (Figure 44).

We have shown photographic evidence that the poster was on display around the country and we have illustrated how it was well known enough at the time to be copied by others. Finally, we have to address the question as to why so few copies of the *London Opinion* poster exist today (possibly less than one dozen) compared with many hundreds of copies of the official PRC posters. Examinations of the recruiting posters in various collections reveal that almost all are in pristine condition, leading to the obvious conclusion that these remaining copies were never used. When the poster campaign fizzled out, the government had thousands of posters on their hands: many were destroyed, many were sent overseas and many were circulated to schools in this country. The popularity of the Kitchener poster and the number of people who saw it obviously cannot be gauged by comparing the number of unused remaining copies. As in any historical debate, lack of documentation for an artefact does not preclude its existence. The worldwide reproduction of the image seems to give every indication that the image was widely known during the war and also that it was seen as a powerful recruiting tool.

One aspect of World War I poster advertising that has received little attention before has become apparent in the research for this book as photographs have come to light of street scenes showing how posters were actually displayed. Contemporary photographs reveal that recruiting posters were often pasted with a number of posters – often identical ones – in the same area, even on the same wall. The result was to reinforce the message, a technique that has been used in advertising over recent years, certainly since US pop artist Andy Warhol used it so effectively in his artwork in the 1950s.

However, there is no indication that this technique was based on theory or in any way suggested by the PRC; one has the impression that the decision to paste up many copies was probably taken by the person who put them up – told to 'paste 'em up on that wall' he (it will undoubtedly have been a 'he' in 1914) probably did just that! There is equally no suggestion that anyone was consciously aware of the powerful effect of using these multiple images. Warhol used this technique in the 1950s to great effect, realising that the same repeated image, particularly of a face, had a powerful effect – emotional as well as visual.

Remember too, that most of these posters were in brilliant colour, not the faded black and white images we see in the old photographs (Figure 52). It is no wonder that people remembered the 'staring face of Kitchener' after being faced by a wall of his staring eyes and his pointing finger – you don't need thousands of individual posters all over the place – one colourful array like this in a prominent place will certainly have a great effect.

Alfred Leete may not have understood the added influence of his image being used in this way and it is certain that the men who posted the bills themselves didn't realise that they were using such an advanced marketing technique.

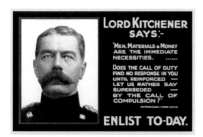

Figure 48. The 'official' Kitchener
poster (1915)

Figure 49. Poster outside of the Bank
of New Zealand in 1915

Figure 50. Recruiting poster, possibly
1915, with the *London Opinion*
artwork

Figure 51. Recruiting poster used in
Canada in 1915

The magic of Leete's poster

Alfred Leete's Kitchener poster has become iconic, not only as an icon of World War I but as an image that demands our attention on several levels and for many reasons. Of course, it is an image with which we are familiar and this must in some way appeal to our senses. Also, the text used requires little change to fit many circumstances. There is another characteristic that is not often appreciated. We are used to posters designed to get us to need the product they depict, whereas this poster reverses this and claims that the object of the poster needs us! However, there is another, far more complex, reason that this image draws us to it, a technique that has been used for almost two millennia by artists and painters to the same ends.

The academic world offers an approach called transactional analysis, which was developed in the 1980s to study communication. This would recognise Kitchener's pointing finger as typical of a 'critical adult', an attitude that requires compliance and is not open to question. Yet, attitudes change over time; a father in the 1950s could wag his finger at a child and say 'You will do it because I say so' (as one of the authors certainly remembers) – but few fathers would get away with this today!

Some commentators would say the strength of the Kitchener image is based on its place in a tradition of classical art and pagan culture. Religious ritual and imagery have supplied the most telling expression of elemental impulses and it may be that pictorial forms are mnemonics for such impulses, which can be transmitted and transformed down the generations. Thus, when we view an image we conjure up past associations and are influenced by them. The Sistine Chapel ceiling by Michelangelo springs to mind (Figure 53).

There are many theories related to posters. According to one academic, William Mitchell:

> 'The picture is a material object, a thing you can burn or break. An image is what appears in a picture, and what survives its destruction – in memory, in narrative and in copies and traces in other media.'

The writer Susan Sontag claims that poster artists are usually plagiarists (whether of their own work or others') and in Picture This, a compilation of writing on World War I posters, Pearl James agrees that posters copy, parody and otherwise repeat eye-catching, memorable and significant images. Back in 1918, Matlack Price and Horace Brown wrote:

> 'The poster must attract attention in the face of a thousand distractions and competitors for attention, and must make itself understood by people who are usually on the move. It calls for a larger size, a forceful use of design and colour and a simple

74

presentation of its message with the medium of print. It must tell its story forcefully and at once. It must be so designed as to be seen in its entirety from a passing vehicle. If the message is rendered in a way too complex for this instantaneous view, there is too much in the design.'

The Leete image's power may stem from many sources. The Italian historian Carlo Ginzburg claims that the Kitchener poster's popularity came from the use of bold colour, and invocation of familiar 'pictorial traditions' that use 'frontal, all seeing figures with fore-shortened pointing fingers' to 'command authority', echoing of art historical tradition, coupled with the sheer number of imitators. The historian Nicholas Hiley leads to a different conclusion. He argues that Leete's image, and the recruitment campaign of which it became part, 'provoked considerable opposition' which was visible precisely through the proliferation of ironic parodies. The fact that the Kitchener poster, he argues, has become an icon of the war tells us not about its success during the recruiting campaign but about its legacies in 'later ironic use'. In his view, we have inherited a myth of the poster's power as a recruiting propaganda tool.

It is arguable that the image itself is strong partly because of subliminal links to classical art: Ginzburg points to the 'Pathosformel' formula of emotion, whereby a form evokes pity or sadness, espoused by the German art historian Aby Warburg: 'It was pagan culture, both in religious ritual and in imagery, that supplied the most telling expression of elemental impulses (Pathosformel). Pictorial forms are mnemonics for such operations; and they can be transmitted, transformed and restored to a new and vigorous life, wherever kindred impulses arise.'

Ginzburg explains that in the thirty-fifth book of *Natural History* – a section devoted to Greek and Roman artists – Pliny the Elder refers to Famulus, a painter from the time of Emperor Augustus: 'To him belonged a [painting of the goddess of wisdom] Minerva who viewed the viewer no matter where he looked from.'

Outside the European classical tradition on the Indian subcontinent, Buddhist caves carved into a hillside at Ajanta cover a period of eight hundred years, starting from the second century BC. The paintings and sculptures are regarded as among the finest surviving examples of Indian art and include faces on ceilings where the subject's eyes follow the viewer around the cave.

Apelles, a fourth-century BC Greek regarded as the greatest painter of antiquity, painted Alexander the Great holding a thunderbolt, in the temple of Artemis at Ephesus, where the figure has 'the appearance of projecting from the surface and the thunderbolt seems to stand out from the picture'. A fourth-century BC Greek artist, Pausias, Pliny continues, invented a method of painting where to show the long body of an ox he painted the animal facing the spectator.

Two millennia later, echoes of these reports can be found in the diaries of Michael MacDonagh in recalling London in January 1915:

'Posters ... Everywhere Lord Kitchener sternly points a monstrously big finger, exclaiming: I Want You.'

Ginzburg quotes Mont Abbott, a young farm-worker from Oxfordshire, writing:

'The gwoost of Kitchener had been fading his finger at me for some time on they washed-out posters outside the Post Office, "Your King and Country NEED YOU".'

Henry Davray, writing in 1916, reinforces the theme:

'The Central Recruiting Committee posted on the walls of London and all over Britain a poster displaying an enormous full-face portrait of Lord Kitchener. From whatever angle it was regarded the eyes met those of the onlooker and never left them; and on one side in large letters was the laconic appeal: Kitchener wants more men.'

These observers may never have read Pliny the Elder, but when we read the words 'from whatever angle [the poster] was regarded, the eyes met those of the onlooker and never left them' we could wonder whose image is being described here, Minerva's or Kitchener's? Whose is the monstrously big finger, Kitchener's or Alexander's?

Referring to De Visione Dei (On the Vision of God) by the German philosopher Nicholas of Cusa (Cusanus) from 1453, Ginzburg explains that to give his readers an idea of the relationship between God and the world, Cusanus wrote that the most appropriate image they could picture would be the face of somebody who sees everything.

In 'Blessing Christ', Antonello da Messina modified the hand by introducing a foreshortening (Figure 54). Much has been written on this, but in the view of Ginzburg he may have been inspired by Pliny's passage on Alexander the Great – the Italian translation appeared in Venice in 1476, about the time Antonello revised his painting. Michelangelo shows an obvious influence in the Sistine Chapel frescos – projecting fingers, gesticulating hands and bold foreshortenings stress spatial and narrative relationships. A similar argument can be used for Pontormo's 'Nude Study' from about 1525 (Figure 55).

We may be able to interpret Kitchener's pointing finger as a secular, foreshortened version of Jesus's horizontal gesture in Caravaggio's 'St Matthew summoned by God'. In both cases we have a call – a call to arms, a religious call. The stern glance, the stabbing finger, the perspective as though seen from below, must have usually elicited a feeling of awe but the poster's aim was to arrest the viewer's attention and bring him to a halt. In 1895, the Lumière brothers had plunged cinema audiences into terror by projecting their film Arrival of a Train into the Station of La

Ciotat. The Kitchener poster relies on the same visual devices and was addressed to an audience becoming familiar to cinema and its visual tricks.

Both Ginzburg and James write that Kitchener must have inspired George Orwell's chilling icon of bureaucratic warmongering, Big Brother in *Nineteen Eighty-Four* (Figure 56). Eric Blair (aka George Orwell) was eleven years old when the war started. In the 1949 novel, the reader is confronted with two descriptions:

'[A] coloured poster, too large for indoor display ··· tacked to the wall. It depicted simply an enormous face, more than a metre wide: the face of a man of about thirty-five, with a heavy black moustache and ruggedly handsome features. It was one of those pictures which are so contrived that the eyes follow you about when you move BIG BROTHER IS WATCHING YOU, the caption beneath it ran.'

'A new poster has suddenly appeared all over London. It had no caption, and represented simply the monstrous figure of a Eurasian soldier, three or four metres high, striding forward with expressionless Mongolian face and enormous boots, a sub-machine gun pointed from his hip. From whatever angle you looked at the poster, the muzzle of the gun, magnified by the foreshortening, seemed to be pointed straight at you.'

One 2004 study, '*Pointing out of the picture*' explains that all it takes for the eyes in an image to follow you round the room is to have the person in the painting, or photograph, look straight ahead, because our visual perception takes care of the rest. The authors describe paintings being ascribed 'almost magical powers' because of the effect and refer to art historian Sir Ernst Gombrich's 1960 study of Leete's poster. The study concludes that 'no special gift or training is involved' and the only 'trick' is to have the subject of the picture to look (and/or point) directly to the lens. The researchers claim that when we observe a picture on a wall the visual information that defines near and far points is unaffected by viewing direction. We interpret this perceptually as if it were a real object, which is why the eyes appear to follow you as you change your viewing direction. This phenomenon is because of the unique perceptual aspects of viewing a picture; we perceive the object depicted in a painting as a surface in three-dimensional space, but we also perceive that the painting is a two-dimensional surface hanging on the wall. Thus, when we look at such a picture, we have these two perceptions simultaneously and it is difficult to make sense of that conceptually – an issue that has fascinated people for hundreds of years.

Even in 1859 this subject was researched by La Gournerie, a French researcher who proposed a mathematical analysis of why eyes in a painting seem to follow viewers. The recent study indicates that La Gournerie had the basic idea right, but his mathematics was wrong – later researchers have provided a better mathematical analysis.

Possibly the best summary of the strengths and weaknesses of Leete's drawing was provided by Maurice Rickards, the graphic designer and ephemera encyclopaedist. He used a simplified version of Leete's Kitchener design as a symbol on the title page of his 1968 book of posters. He sums up the power of the image:

> 'Your Country Needs YOU is by no means a major work, but its posterly simplicity has impact far in excess of any of its contemporaries. His lordship's accusing finger has haunted Britons since they first saw it. It is the archetype of all wartime father figures, crib-source for a host of mimics. Like the man himself – brooding, compulsive and final – it has entered into the mythology of the nation; it has become a trade-mark figure for World War I. In a multitude of contexts, sacred and profane, it has been revived in parody. In the wave of mock nostalgia that swept the last of the nineteen-sixties, the image was again revived – this time as a pop-art decoration piece. Kitchener ⋯ would have been greatly mystified.'

Such a wave of mock nostalgia would see the poster 'Keep Calm and Carry On' establish a similar popularity after 2000. Like the Leete design, it comes with its own mis-remembered history, for, having been intended as a poster to bolster morale in the event of a wartime disaster, it was never actually used. Instead, its utility is based on treating austerity with nostalgic irony. Paul Atterbury, a specialist on the BBC television programme Antiques Roadshow, wrote to the authors to make an interesting point:

> 'Some time ago a national newspaper published an article stating that there was only one surviving original Keep Calm and Carry On poster and it was in the Imperial War Museum and priceless. Well, I have one on my wall, and we had a lady on the Roadshow a couple of years ago with seventeen. So they are rare, but there are probably quite a few out there.

> 'They were all issued to post offices and government buildings during the summer of 1940, ready to be displayed if required. Unused, most were simply thrown away. The survivors probably lurked forgotten at the back of cupboards. Mine was a present years ago from a lady whose family had run a village post office. They had found a few during a recent clear out. The seventeen on the Roadshow were a similar story, found rolled up in a cupboard years after the war.'

Figure 52. Simulation in colour of a bus outside Chester Station (1915)

Figure 53. Detail from the Sistine Chapel 'Creation of the Sun and Moon' by
Michelangelo (1508–12)

How did Leete's image stay in the memory?

London Opinion carried Alfred Leete's Lord Kitchener for the first time on 5 September 1914 and by the next issue was selling postcards of the cover at 1s 4d for a hundred. By the end of the month the design was being issued as a private poster and the Parliamentary Recruiting Committee obtained permission to use it with amended text. Leete produced a parody for a later *London Opinion* cover, showing the long arm of Kitchener with 'Conscription' written on the sleeve, reaching out to grab a man reading a paper. The magazine continued as one of the best-selling weeklies, but was ultimately merged into *Men Only*, which was owned by the same publisher, in 1954 as the general men's magazine marker contracted. Yet, as this chapter will demonstrate, the fame of the Kitchener poster meant that it was kept in the minds of the population through memory, exhibitions, journalism, parody and by being exploited as a marketing tool.

In March 1917, the war cabinet approved an idea from Sir Alfred Mond MP to create a national war museum that would record the events of, and curate objects from, the Great War. The intention was to collect and display material as a record of everyone's experiences during the war – civilian and military – and to commemorate the sacrifices of all sections of society. Because of interest from countries in the empire, it was later renamed the Imperial War Museum. The IMW has always claimed to have purchased the artwork but recent research by James Taylor indicates that the artwork may have been one of four drawings donated to the IWM by Leete himself in 1917, indeed Taylor claims that they were incorrectly catalogued at the time of acquisition.

One of the museum's first exhibitions was held in 1918 in Burlington House in London. The event hosted objects and photographs from the war, with rooms devoted to New Zealand, Australia, Britain, the Air Ministry, Canada, Royal Academy pictures and women's work. Posters were displayed in the vestibule and, although the published catalogue listing the objects and photographs in the exhibition, it unfortunately did not include the posters displayed. However, the Mary Evans Picture Library reckons the Leete posters were not displayed, though one of them did feature in an exhibition at the Grafton Galleries in 1919.

The online archive for *Hansard*, the record of parliamentary debates in both the House of Lords and the House of Commons, provides an interesting pattern in terms of use of the phrase 'Your country needs you.' It is not recorded in the nineteenth century and comes up first in 1915 when an MP quotes a recruitment poster. It then appears twenty times more in the 1900s, although not in either the Twenties or Fifties. In the new millennium, it has been voiced just once, in 2004.

Going back to that parliamentary coinage, in June 1915, an MP says: 'Here is a poster I got from the recruiting committee. It says, "Your country needs you." It represents a Highlander gazing down upon a village, and underneath are the words, "Is not this worth fighting for?"' This is the first time Hansard has the phrase being spoken. It is used again in 1916 and 1919, but then does not crop up again until the 1930s, when it is usually used in debates about the sacrifice people made in the Great War and the way the phrase gave people a stake in the country.

The Kitchener poster made a mark on the generation that saw it, as Michael MacDonagh recalled in his diaries, which were published in 1935:

> 'Posters appealing to recruits are to be seen on every hoarding, in most windows, tramcars and commercial vans. The great base of Nelson's Pillar is covered with them. Their number and variety are remarkable. Everywhere Lord Kitchener sternly points a monstrously big finger, exclaiming "I Want You."'

The *Daily Mail* reported General Sir Arthur Currie, the principal of McGill University, using the phrase 'Your country needs you' in a February 1927 address to students urging them to stay in Canada and not be lured to the US.

Another set of memoirs, *Great Event*, by Horace Buckley, a former lieutenant in the Coldstream Guards, is described in an advert in the *Times* of 28 November 1930 as 'An honest, balanced story of a public school boy's war experiences from the moment he saw the poster Kitchener Wants You!'

In 1931, the Victoria & Albert Museum held an exhibition of 450 posters from around the world, of which about half were from Britain. Several posters from the Great War were shown, including two by Frank Brangwyn and one by Paul Nash. The Leete poster was not among them, but this could be as the focus of the exhibition was the art of the poster and, from the museum's point of view, it was as much about colour lithographic printing as posters. From an artistic viewpoint, Leete's image would not have been a match for these as its power lies elsewhere. Work from the US was included, including seven from the war, but Flagg's recruitment posters were not shown.

Early in the Second World War, Leete's artwork was dusted off for the cover of Picture Post. Under Hungarian-born photojournalist Stefan Lorant, who had fled to London after being imprisoned by Hitler, and his deputy Tom Hopkinson, this large format weekly had become one of the best-selling magazines in the country, with sales of close to two million copies. The issue appeared in the same week as the Dunkirk rescue of June 1940 and, if Leete's image was in any danger of being forgotten before, it was certainly back in the public eye now.

Figure 54. Antonello da Messina's 'Blessing Christ' (c1465)

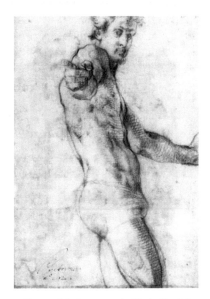

Figure 55. Pontormo's 'Nude Study' creates intimacy between the painter's self image and the viewer (c1525)

Figure 56. Still from Nineteen Eighty-Four based on George Orwell's novel

Figure 57. The poster technique used to good effect by Margaret Thatcher (1982)

In parliament, Eleanor Rathbone, MP for the Combined English Universities in December 1941, referred back to the Great War in a debate about how to appeal to women for war work:

'The adventurous note is not really the best way to catch the best brains among women. The underlying motive can be expressed in the oldest of all appeals, "Your country needs you."'

As for the government's slogans of the day, the *Daily Mail*'s George Murray attacked them as 'like a slab of cold pudding'. Comparing them with the Great War's efforts, he said:

'Your country needs you ⋯ From ten thousand hoardings the compelling finger of Kitchener pointed straight to the passers-by. There was no escaping it. That poster of the last war sticks in my mind today. I can't forget it. But what's the slogan of this war? I see one six times a day – but I can't remember it. I have to write it down. Here it is: "Your courage, your cheerfulness, your resolution will bring us victory".'

In a similar vein, after the war, in 1949, Totnes MP Ralph Rayner, who had fought in the first war, also castigated the efforts of poster writers:

'There is also a lack of guts about our slogans. I cannot remember one of them. In the last war, that finger of Lord Kitchener, pointing at one from every hoarding, touched one right on the solar plexus. That curt injunction, "Your country needs you," made every man want to do his damnedest. I do not know whether the long lull is responsible for the failure of inspiration on the part of our inventors of slogans.'

Leete's artwork was on show again at a display of old army recruitment posters held at Charing Cross Underground station and reported on in the *Times* in November 1949. The picture caption read: 'The Kitchener poster seen above was well known in the 1914-18 war' and the artwork appears to have been given pride of place in the exhibit. Another prominent outing was as one of the eight images on the cover of a magazine published by the Daily Telegraph to celebrate the newspaper's centenary in 1955. It was repeated as a quarter-page inside and also identified as a poster. In 1953, a Britannia class locomotive was named Lord Kitchener, joining other war heroes Lord Roberts, under whom Kitchener served in the second Boer war, and Lord Haig, who had taken over leadership of the British Expeditionary Force from Sir John French in 1915.

In 1958, Philip Magnus's Kitchener: *Portrait of an Imperialist* was published with a jacket design by Osbert Lancaster, one of Britain's best-known illustrators, who had pioneered the pocket cartoon at the *Daily Express* during the Second World War (Figure 58). The Lancaster jacket portrays Kitchener in a tarboosh (fez) as a 'pasha', an honorary title in Egypt equivalent to a British lord. The biography identifies Leete's artwork as the poster, with no reference to *London Opinion*. The book reproduced on a full page the Leete image with a credit to the Imperial War Museum and the caption: 'Recruiting poster, 1914, designed by Alfred Leete.' Magnus describes how:

> 'The whole country was soon placarded with posters depicting Kitchener in the character of Big Brother, with a field marshal's cap, hypnotic eyes, bristling moustache, pointing finger and the legend "Your Country Needs YOU". Volunteers thereafter flowed in at a rate which strained almost to breaking-point the hastily improvised machinery for accommodating, equipping and training them.'

Magnus also repeated one of the best quotations about Kitchener, though without identifying the source:

> 'Mrs Asquith remarked indiscreetly that if Kitchener was not a great man, he was, at least, a great poster; and Kitchener retorted by telling his personal staff that all his colleagues repeated military secrets to their wives, except Asquith, who repeated them to other people's wives.'

Under the headline 'Doing what comes naturally' the *Daily Mail* ran a picture caption story about a 1959 recruiting film for the Women's Royal Army Corps in which; 'With the impact of the Kitchener poster two wars ago, Private Wallis marches up to the camera for 20 seconds ⋯ and salutes.' 'No Guards could better it,' said experts.'

Clearly, the *Daily Mail* expected its readers to understand the Kitchener poster reference, even though it dated back forty-five years.

The 'your country' phrase again crops up in parliament in 1960, when an MP tells the Commons: 'Your country needs you in the teaching profession.'

A July 1961 column in the *Daily Mail* gives an example of Leete's image being used in a mocking way (Figure 59). Harold Macmillan, the prime minister, is ridiculed with the words:

> 'We could do another version of that famous Kitchener poster of the First World War which haunted the column-dodgers and stay-at-homes with its staring eyes and pointing finger. Today the awkward question would be – 'But Does the Country Need YOU?'

It was accompanied by a sketch of the idea. And the thrust of that column is picked up a year later by an MP criticising the level of service pension. Commander Harry Pursey, who had started as a boy seaman and fought at the Battle of Jutland, cries: 'The minister of defence should have his photograph taken for a recruiting poster, in the pose of Kitchener in the First World War, pointing his finger and saying, "Your Country Needs You," with a second slogan "See the World at Government Expense – and after 25 years' service return to National Assistance."'

On a totally different tack, in 1962, Jump Up, an Island Records label, released '*Love in the Cemetery*', the first of several singles by a Jamaican reggae/calypso band called Lord Kitchener. A later single was '*Dr Kitch*'.

But the biggest outing of the period for the pointing Kitchener was yet to come. It was as an icon of the Swinging Sixties – a usage by an anti-establishment youth throwing off the grey austerity years of the previous decade that would shock the older generation. I was Lord Kitchener's Valet was a boutique in London's Portobello Road and then Carnaby Street. The shop claimed to be London's first second-hand shop, selling 'kinky, period and military gear' such as uniforms, silk shirts and 'pop art' Union flags. Robert Orbach, a director of the shop, says the name was thought up by Ian Fisk, one of the founders:

> '... just because we sold Victoriana. It conjured up images of Edwardian smoking jackets, top hats and canes and Birdcage Walk on Sunday – pure nostalgia. All of a sudden more people were in there than in the rest of Carnaby Street. With incense burning, it was great, like paradise, you didn't know who was going to walk through the door.'

Eric Clapton bought a military jacket early in 1966 and was soon followed by John Lennon, Mick Jagger and Cynthia Lennon. Jagger bought a red Grenadier guardsman drummer's jacket and wore it on ITV's Ready Steady Go when the Rolling Stones performed '*Paint it Black*'; next morning there were queues around the block. The shop's sign – a rendition of Leete's image in colour by painter Pat Hartnet – has been credited with inspiring pop artists Peter Blake and Jann Haworth with the idea for the uniforms on the Beatles' Sgt Pepper's album. Hartnet's painting is held by the V&A Museum.

Officers' tunics dating from the Great War sold by Lord Kitchener's Valet became an essential component of the Psychedelic style and were also worn by both the Beatles and Jimi Hendrix. The shop became an influential venue and featured in many contemporary documentary photographs and film footage. *Men Only* magazine ran a feature about the boutique in its May 1967 issue. The Kitchener image was also used on colour posters promoting Carnaby Street to tourists. The military look appeared again in the 1980s, with singers such as new romantic Adam Ant wearing military garb.

In the US, the Flagg derivative of Leete's drawing was used for similarly rebellious purposes in the form of propaganda against the Vietnam war.

In 1968, the Leete poster was revived for another purpose, but one that might have met with more sympathy from Kitchener himself. The Back Britain campaign aimed to encourage people to buy domestic goods. Posters went up on 17,000 hoardings with Kitchener on a Union flag background, but with the challenging finger turned around and the caption: 'I'm backing Britain – Will you?' For the columnist Anne Scott-James writing in the *Daily Mail* the next day the campaign was creepy:

> 'To invoke Lord Kitchener – an arch imperialist, a foul personality, a man who quarrelled with politicians, viceroys, officers and men, and who had the Mahdi's head made into an inkstand – is to revive the crassest attitudes of World War I.' 'Let's hope the Kitchener campaign will be laughed out of court, for the British have grown up since 1914 and remained wonderfully civilised through all the agonies of World War II.'

Scott-James was one of Fleet Street's most experienced journalists, having been woman's editor on *Picture Post* during the war, editor of Harper's Bazaar and a star columnist on the *Sunday Express*. She was married to Osbert Lancaster, who had designed the jacket for Magnus's 1959 Kitchener biography. Her mention of the Mahdi's head refers to the 1899 controversy over Kitchener having the body of Mohammed Ahmed, leader of the Sudan uprising, taken from its tomb and thrown into the Nile. The desecration was defended on the grounds that a cult might grow up around the grave and lead to another uprising. The *Guardian* condemned the action. Others interpreted it as revenge for the 1895 beheading of General Gordon in Khartoum, hence the nickname 'Avenger of Gordon'. Magnus describes how the 'great howl of rage' in the press over the skull being taken caused Kitchener to write to Queen Victoria expressing his regret at any distress he had caused and saying: 'I had thought of sending [the head] to the College of Surgeons where, I believe, such things are kept. It has now been buried in a Moslem cemetery.'

The 'Your Country Needs You' phrase was also called up to appeal for more exports (1975), to encourage people to holiday at home (1989) and as part of an attack against the profligate cost of the Conservative government's publicity campaigns to encourage privatisation (1989).

On 1 February 1980, Jonathan Aitken, the Conservative MP who would later be jailed for perjury and perverting the course of justice after claiming to wield the 'sword of truth' against the *Guardian* newspaper, puts his own version of history on the parliamentary record:

> 'My honourable friend the member for Woking made a ringing cry for a register of volunteers. We have tried that once this century, and it was a disaster. It may be that in the rosy hue of historical memory one thinks of Kitchener's efforts to raise volunteer armies as a great success. In a way, it was. A poster saying "your country needs you", with a good photograph, encouraged more than two million men to register for the Colours. But one tends to forget more than sixty years later that Lord Kitchener's nickname at the time was "K of chaos", because the volunteer armies led to far greater muddle and inefficiency and, incidentally, created a much

nastier atmosphere with young girls presenting white feathers to men who had tried to enrol but could not do so. The volunteer system of call-up failed in the First World War and, in the end, it had to be replaced by national service and conscription.'

Notice the description of the photograph with the phrase, a version of events that encapsulates the way people have confused the many versions of the Kitchener poster.

A better gloss on the slogan was provided by Maurice Saatchi, one of the founders of Saatchi & Saatchi, the advertising agency that created the 1979 general election poster for the Tories attacking their great rivals, 'Labour isn't working'. In a 1996 Lords debate on the role of the media in a democratic society, Lord Saatchi tells the house:

> 'The great communicators in history have always made things simple: "Your country needs you", "No taxation without representation" or, "One man, one vote". These are not just slogans; they encapsulate whole philosophies, aspirations and political systems.'

Two years later, the V&A Museum returned to the subject of posters, hosting an exhibition and publishing an accompanying book by Margaret Timmers, *The Power of the Poster*. The book makes reference to research by the government into the best type of posters just before the start of the Second World War, when a member of the public suggests the text-only posters would be enlivened by an image and cites the example of the Kitchener posters.

The Army Careers Office also returned to the iconic Leete image in the late 1990s, but replaced Kitchener's face with that of a young black man. According to the V&A Museum, which holds a copy of the poster, it was directed at Britain's black and Asian communities. Following accusations of racism within the forces in the mid-1990s, the new Labour government insisted on a proactive recruitment campaign and percentage quota targets. This contributed to a slow rise in the number of ethnic minority recruits; from less than one per cent in 1996-97 to about two per cent in 1999-2000, and almost six per cent in 2002.

As technology made it cheaper and quicker to reproduce images, with cheaper printing and photocopiers, and then widespread computers and the web, Leete's image was increasingly used for a wide variety of purposes, from publicising village fetes to jumble sales and garage sales. Alongside these amateur examples, newspapers such as the *Daily Mirror* used it to celebrate the expected victory of Tony Blair in the 1997 election and, after David Cameron evoked the 'Your country needs you' mantra to launch his 'Big Society' idea in 2010, the *Sunday Times* overlaid the prime minister's face on the Leete image. In between these uses, in 1999, the advertising industry magazine Campaign identified Leete's Kitchener poster as the second best poster of the century after Saatchi & Saatchi's 'Labour isn't working'.

Three years later, the same magazine nominated the Leete poster as 'the best recruitment advert of all time'. Eric Field was identified as the copywriter, Leete the illustrator and Caxton the agency for the various versions.

Such was the fame of the poster that it was the subject of many articles and television programmes, including a History Channel documentary, *A Small Piece of History*, in 2003.

To promote the launch of its online archive of articles going back to 1785, the publisher of the *Times* and *Sunday Times* turned to Leete's Kitchener image alongside an illustration of the sinking Titanic for its promotional material.

And Leete's image, or variations on his theme, has been seen on many magazine covers since the start of the new century. These include titles as varied as *Dr Who Magazine*, *Brain Damage*, the *Economist*, *Radio Times* and *Military History*.

The fifth edition of the book *Propaganda and Persuasion* by two US academics, Garth Jowett and Victoria O'Donnell, uses a derivative of the Leete image on the cover but, strangely, does not mention Leete in its index. And the British Library reproduced Leete's image on its souvenirs for the 2013 exhibition Propaganda: Power and Persuasion, though it used one of the early derivatives, James Montgomery Flagg's Uncle Sam variant, for the main promotional posters, presumably because of its more colourful artwork.

Just as in the Victorian and Edwardian eras, a souvenir industry built up around Kitchener is very much alive and well. Tea-towels, cushions, mugs, badges, posters, mouse mats, watches, wash bags, T-shirts and mobile phone covers can be brought on the web and in shops based on copies of, or redrawings of, Leete's rendition of the military hero. Many of these are humorous, such as 'I want you to pull my finger' or 'Your pub needs you' but just as many celebrate Kitchener as a historic figure or mark the war. In 1999, Royal Doulton issued a limited edition jug to mark the sesquicentenary of Kitchener's birth, with the handle depicting poppies and a version of the poster. How many of today's household names will be celebrated in such a way one a century from now?

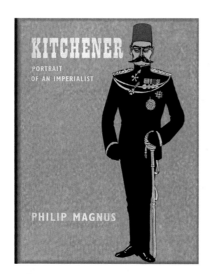

Figure 58. Jacket design by Osbert
Lancaster of Kitchener Pasha

Figure 59. The *Daily Mail* ridicules
Harold Macmillan, the prime minister
(1961)

Figure 60. Sky TV advertisement for
Meet the Chickens (2013)

What is the truth?

Recollections of events and situations that occurred nearly a century ago can be remote from actuality. The aim of this book has not been to credit or discredit the claims of others but to bring together the theories that have been proposed over the years and review them using as much original material as possible. The result is the most complete and up to date picture of the events and life of this iconic poster.

There is little doubt that the 'Kitchener' poster is an icon of the First World War. The words on the poster were both 'Britons. [Kitchener] Wants You' and the more referred to 'Your Country Needs You', which appeared on the front of the *London Opinion* in 1914 and later on a poster by the printer David Allen.

We have referred to claims about the exposure and effectiveness of the Leete poster during the war. Added to the fact that it seems not to have been officially sanctioned, and that there are no contemporary records of its use or effect as a recruiting aid, there was another, official Kitchener poster with an image of the great man. So it is easy to arrive at the conclusion that the Leete poster may have been a bit on a non-event. However, as we have shown, there is evidence that it was well known at the time and, indeed, it was copied by other nations.

At the end of the Great War, if not before, all posters will have been removed and within a few years faded in the public's mind as happier days seemed to lie ahead. The poster based on Alfred Leete's artwork was not one of the most numerous of the recruiting posters; in fact, it is well down the scale in terms of numbers printed. However, this poster, out of hundreds of others, has survived in the collective memory and it alone has become an icon of World War One.

Alfred Leete may have based his image on a contemporary cigarette advertisement but all graphic designers exploit previous images. Indeed, the technique of direct eyes has been used in religious and other paintings to good effect for millennia and few people observing the poster would have failed, consciously or sub-consciously, to have made a connection between Kitchener and God. Similarly, the foreshortened arm to link observer and image has been used to powerful effect in religious paintings. The exaggerated black moustache in the very centre of the image draws attention to the poster and the position of the face in the middle of the frame mimics religious iconography. Leete, knowingly or unknowingly, brought together some of the most powerful techniques of artists throughout history to force the observer to feel the effect of his design.

The poster campaign eventually fizzled out. By 1916 the British public was skilled in resisting the power of commercial advertising and simply transferred to the recruiting campaign the ironic detachment that had developed from years of exposure to the inflated claims of products such as Rowntree's Cocoa, Pears' Soap and Coleman's Mustard. However, if we detach ourselves from the horrors of the war and concentrate on the graphic design, the recruiting campaign produced colourful imagery that has remained with us and certainly influenced design today.

This powerful sketch by Leete was said to have been completed within a day. The result – the poster 'Your Country Needs You' – is now famous and part of our 'mental furniture'. A century later, Kitchener is better known for his image on a poster than for his martial pursuits. Within a few years of the poster's appearance, the comment

'A poor general, but a wonderful poster' was supposedly made of him. In our minds we associate Leete's image and words with World War I and it has been assimilated into our own partial vision of the conflict. None of us is sure whether it is the eyes, the finger or the words themselves; we don't know if it is the image or the associations connected to it that stir us, but the effect remains as powerful today as it obviously was a century ago – so much so that the image, almost unaltered, has been re-used thousands of times over the years and no doubt will continue to inspire people, knowingly or unwittingly, for decades to come.

Figure 61. Leete's iconic Kitchener poster

Acknowledgements

The authors wish to thank:

Atterbury Paul; for permission to use email content.

Cheltenham Art Gallery for permission to use the A. Davies portrait of Lord Kitchener

Great War Forum members for three years of advice and support (www.1914-1918.net)

Imperial War Museum London for permission to use original Leete artwork (IWM_PST_002735) and the poster (IWM_PST_0414)

James Taylor, author of Your Country Needs You

McMaster University, Hamilton, for permission to quote from the online article 'Peace and war in the 20th century'

National Portrait Gallery for permission to use Kitchener portrait (MW112299)

National Railway Museum, Science & Society Picture Library for permission to use the photograph of Liverpool Exchange Station

Nicholas Hiley: permission to quote from his essay 'Kitchener Wants You and Daddy what did YOU do in the Great War?: the myth of British recruiting posters' Imperial War Museum Review, No. 11

Oxford University Press and History Workshop Journal for permission to quote from 'Your Country Needs You: a case study in political iconography' by Carlo Ginzburg

Paul Rennie, Head of Context in Graphic Design at Central St Martins permission to quote from a lecture.

Richard Slocombe, senior curator of art at the Imperial War Museum

SB Publications for permission to use images of Chester from Chester vol 2 portrait in old Picture Postcards by Goulborn and Jackson

Lady Kenya Tatton-Brown (nee Kitchener) permission to quote a private conversation.

University of Nebraska for permission for permission to quote from 'Picture this. WWI posters and visual culture', 2009

List of illustrations

Bibliography

Advertisement for Great Event, by Horace Buckley (1930) *Times*, November 28. 22

Albrinck M. (2009) 'Humanitarians and he-men: recruitment, posters and the masculine ideal imaginings of war' in James P. (ed) Picture This: World War I Posters and Visual Culture, University of Nebraska

Allen W.E.D. (1957) David Allens: The history of a family firm 1857-1957. London: John Murray

Anon. (1914) 'Lord Haldane or Lord Kitchener?' *Times*, 5 August. 7

Anon. (1914) 'War Comments', *Bystander*, 16 September. 536

Anon. (1914) 'Uniformed already – and reviewed', *Bystander*, 30 September. 601

Anon. (1914) L'Illustration, 21 October 1914

Anon. (1914) 'What damps recruiting ardour' (cartoon), *Bystander*, 14 November. 19

Anon. (1915) 'Lord Kitchener and the Suffragists', *Times*, 25 January. 5

Anon. (1916) 'The memorial service for Lord Kitchener', Sphere, 17 June. 244-252

Anon. (1949) 'Picture Gallery', *Times*, 22 November. 10

Anon. (1959) 'Doing what comes naturally', *Daily Mail*, 5 February. 2

Anon. (1961) 'The same old clichés won't do this time, Harold', *Daily Mail*, 14 July. 8

Anon. (1968) 'I'm backing Britain – Will You?' *Daily Mail*, 24 January. 7

Anon. (1999) 'Poster advertising awards 1999 (poster of the century)', Campaign, 15 October

Anon. (2002) 'The 10 best recruitment ads of all time', Campaign, 17 December. 9

Anon. (accessed August 2013) 'History: Cases from the National Archives – Carl Hans Lody'. www.mi5.gov.uk/home/mi5-history/mi5s-early-years/carl-hans-lody.html

Asquith H.H. (1921) 'An appreciation of Lord Kitchener', *Pearsons*, December (continued in Feb 1922)

Aulich J. and Hewitt J. (2007) Seduction or Instruction? First World War posters in Britain and Europe. Manchester University Press

Bairnsfather B. (1915) 'Where did that one go to?' (cartoon). *Bystander*, 31 March. 458

Baumer L. (1916) 'Mr *Punch*'s wartime revue' (cartoon). *Punch*, 5 July. 22-3

Brex T. (1914) Scare-mongerings from the '*Daily Mail*' 1896-1914: The paper that foretold the war. London: *Daily Mail*

Bridgewater H. (1910) Advertising; or, the art of making known. London: Pitman

Browne T. (1910) In Other People's Shoes. London: Lang

Bryant E.M. (1915) 'His call to Arms', Windsor, May. 41

Buckley H.H.C (1930) Great Event. London: Figurehead

Buller T.F. (1971) O'r Wyrcws I Baradwys. Dinbych, Denbigh: Gwasg Gee

Cartoon Archive, University of Kent, www.cartoons.ac.uk

Daily Telegraph (1955) 'Britain at War: Kitchener's call for recruits', 100 Years in Pictures: Centenary supplement to the Daily Telegraph. 42

Dark S. (1922) The Life of Sir Arthur Pearson. London: Hodder & Stoughton

Darracott J. and Loftus B. (1972) First World War Posters. London: Imperial War Museum

Davies R. (1990) Ronald Searle. London: Sinclair-Stevenson

Davray H.D. (1916) Lord Kitchener: His work and his prestige. London: T. Fisher Unwin

Denny F. (2013) Encyclopædia of the British Music Hall. www.oldtimemusichall.net/chirgwin.htm

Dodds E. (1918) 'The all clear boys', *Pearsons*, August. 96-7

Dudley A. (1916) Valediction: Sonnets to Kitchener. London: Arthur L. Humphreys

Esher R. (1921) The Tragedy of Lord Kitchener. London: John Murray

Field E. (1914) 'What the Army offers' (advertisement), *Daily Mail*, 15 January. 1

Field E. (1959) Advertising: The forgotten years. London: Ernest Benn

'Fougasse' (Cyril Bird) (1916) 'War's brutalising influence' (cartoon) *Punch*, 19 July. 53

Gaunt W. (1961) 'Posters as an Open Air Art Gallery', *Times*, 21 June. 13

Gifford D. (2004) Obituary: Norman Thelwell, Guardian, 10 February. 25

Ginzburg C. (2001) 'Your country needs you: a case study in political iconography', History Workshop Journal. No. 52

Gombrich E.E. (1960) Art and Illusion. A study of the psychology of pictorial representation. London: Phaidon

Graves C. (1939) 'I see Life' (Sandy's Autograph Bar), *Daily Mail*, 28 February. 8

Hall S.R. (1915) Writing an Advertisement. Boston, MA: Houghton Mifflin

Hardie M. & Sabin A.K. (1920) War Posters Issued by Belligerent and Neutral Nations 1914-1919. London: A. & C. Black

Henty G.A. (1903) With Kitchener in the Soudan: A story of Atbara and Omdurman. London: Blackie

Hickling P.B. (1915) 'During a Zeppelin raid' (cartoon), *Punch*, 17 November. 405

Hiley N. (1987) 'Sir Hedley Le Bas and the origins of domestic propaganda in Britain 1914-17', European Journal of Marketing, Vol. 21 No. 8. 30-46

Hiley N. (1997) 'Kitchener Wants You and Daddy what did YOU do in the Great War?: the myth of British recruiting posters' in Smith J. & Simkins P. (eds) Imperial War Museum Review. No. 11

History Channel (2003) A Small Piece of History, 16 February

James P. (ed.) (2009) Picture This: World War I posters and visual culture, University of Nebraska

Jones-Edwards W. (1963) Ar Lethrau Ffair Rhos. Aberystwyth: Atgofion Mwnwr, Cymdeithas Lyfrau Ceredigion Gyf

Jowett G.S. and O'Donnell V.J. (2012) Propaganda and Persuasion. New York: Sage

Kirkwood P.M. (2012) 'The impact of fiction on public debate in late Victorian Britain: the Battle of Dorking and the "lost career" of Sir George Tomkyns Chesney', Graduate History Review. Vol. 4, no. 1

Koenderink J.J., van Doorn A.J., Kappers A.M.L. and Todd J.T. (2004) 'Pointing out of the picture.' Perception. No, 33. 513-169

Laffin J. (2011) Tommy Atkins: The story of the English soldier. Stroud: History Press

Le Bas H.F. (1917) Lord Kitchener Memorial Book. London: Hodder and Stoughton

Leete A. (1914) 'Get out and get under' (cartoon). *Bystander*, 26 August. 439

Leete A. (1929) 'Mr York of York, Yorks' (animated commercial). British Publicity Talking Films for Rowntree. http://yorkshirefilmarchive.com/film/mr-york-york-yorks

Levine J. (2008) Forgotten Voices of the Somme. London: Ebury Press

MacDonagh M. (1935) In London During the Great War: The diary of a journalist. London: Eyre and Spottiswoode

Magnus P. (1958) Kitchener: Portrait of an Imperialist. London: John Murray

Macqueen-Pope W. (1957) 'Personalities of the old London office', in Allen W.E.D. 208-17

Messinger G.S. (1992) British Propaganda and the State in the First World War. Manchester University Press

Mitchell W.J.T. (2008) 'Visual literacy or literary visualcy?', in Elkins J. (ed) Visual Literacy. New York: Routledge

Murray G. (1940) 'Should they put a laugh in the "don't-talk" drive?', *Daily Mail*. 7 February. 6

Norton J.S. (1918) The Kitchener Birthday Book. London: Samson Low, Marston

Orbach R. (2006) 'Interview with Robert Orbach', V&A transcript, February. www.vam.ac.uk/content/articles/i/robert-orbach/

Orwell G. (1949) Nineteen Eighty-Four. London: Secker & Warburg

Partridge B. (1916) 'The lost chief' (cartoon) *Punch*, 14 June. 393

De Pereot M. (1914) 'French soldiers' wives in London', *Daily Mail*, Letters, 22 October. 4

Pincas S. and Loiseau M. (2006) A History of Advertising. Cologne: Taschen

Perisco J. (2004) Eleventh Month, Eleventh Day, Eleventh Hour: Armistice Day, 1918. New York: Random House

Price M. and Brown H. (1918) How to Put in Patriotic Posters the Stuff that Makes People Stop, Look, Act, National Committee of Patriotic Societies, Washington

Quinn A. (2008) 'London Opinion – the most influential cover', www.magforum.com/mens/london-opinion.htm

Quinn A. (2014) British Magazine Design Since 1840. London: V&A Publishing

Quinn A. (2013) 'Magazines and periodicals' in Cambridge History of the Book in Britain, vol. 7. Cambridge University Press

Rees N. (2011) Don't You Know There's a War On? London: Batsford

Richardson M. (2000) The Tigers. Barnsley: Pen and Sword Books

Rickards M. (1968) Posters of the First World War. London: Evelyn, Adams & Mackay

Rigney F. (1914) 'The change in Ireland' (cartoon). Bystander, 19 August. 413

Saunders N.J. (2001) Trench Art: A brief guide and history. Barnsley: Leo Cooper

Scott-James A. (1968) 'Anne Scott-James' column, Daily Mail, 25 January. 6

Simkins P. (1988) Kitchener's Army: The raising of the new armies 1914-1916. Manchester University Press

Slocombe R. (2010) Interview with the senior curator of art at the Imperial War Museum, July

Sontag S. (1970) 'Introduction' in Stermer D., The Art of Revolution: Castro's Cuba 1959-1970. New York: McGraw-Hill

'Spy'(Leslie Ward) (1899) 'Khartoum' (cartoon). Vanity Fair, 23 February

Steevens G.W. (1898) With Kitchener to Khartum. Edinburgh: William Blackwood

Straus R. (1914) 'Armageddon – in prophecy. How near scare-fictionists have come to the truth'. Bystander, 19 August. 429-30

Taylor J. (2013) Your Country Needs You: The secret history of the ultimate propaganda poster. Glasgow: Saraband

Thatcher M. (2011) Myth and Magic: An essay on the iconic Kitchener poster. Chester: Funfly Design

Thomas B. (1915) 'The tolerated tiger' (cartoon). London Opinion, 20 March. 33

Thomas B. (1916) 'A fair exchange' (cartoon). London Opinion, 26 August. 93

Thomas B. and Williams W. with Lincoln Springfield (1919) One Hundred War Cartoons from 'London Opinion'. London: London Opinion

Timmers M. (1988) The Power of the Poster. London: V&A Publications

Todd J., Koenderink J., van Doorn A., and Kappers A. (1996) 'Effects of changing viewing conditions on the perceived structure of smoothly curved surfaces', Journal of Experimental Psychology: Human Perception and Performance, vol. 27 no.3, 695-706

Townsend W.H. (1911) 'Kindred spirits' (cartoon). Punch, 20 September

V&A (2002) Posters Study Guide (Bibliography), 1 August. www.vam.ac.uk/content/articles/p/study-guide-posters

Warby M. (2013) www.brucebairnsfather.org.uk

Watkins O.S (1899) With Kitchener's Army: Being a chaplain's experiences with the Nile expedition, 1898. London: S.W. Partridge

Winter J. (2009) 'Imaginings of war: posters and the shadow of the lost generation' in James P. (ed.) Picture This: World War I posters and visual culture, University of Nebraska

Woolrich E.F. (1914) 'There is time to finish the game' (cartoon). Bystander, 19 August. 411

Index

The Authors

Martyn Thatcher has an Honours degree in Graphic Design and Interactive Media and is currently the joint proprietor of Funfly Design (with his wife). He originally researched the Kitchener poster as a degree dissertation and in 2011 published a book on the subject. He has also written about Andy Warhol. Martyn is a qualified pilot, a musician and keen golfer. Although his accent betrays his West Country origins he currently lives in Cheshire.

Anthony Quinn is a Fellow of the RSA and a senior journalist on a national newspaper and former head of the School of Publishing at West Herts College in Watford. He has served as an external examiner in publishing and journalism for Kingston University and the London ication. His books include British Magazine Design Since 1840 (2014 by V&A Publications) and the Pira Guide to CD-ROM (Pira International, 1996); he also contributed the chapter 'Magazines since 1914', in the Cambridge History of the Book in Britain (vol 7) from Cambridge University Press. He holds a degree in Engineering Science from Warwick University. He hails from Liverpool and lives in Hadleigh, Suffolk, and London.

Funfly Design was started in 1996 and is the studio name of Martyn, who specialises in publishing and graphic gesign and his wife Patricia, a metalworker and enamellist. It is a family business dedicated to quality work. www.funfly.co.uk.

Magforum.com is a website about the past, present and future of magazines and publishing. The site was founded in 2001 by Anthony Quinn, who, from 1999, had published similar pages as head of Watford School of Publishing at West Herts College. www.magforum.com.

Please send us a message if you enjoyed the book - we love to hear from you. You can do this via our our website at www.kitchenerposter.co.uk.

We do hope that you have enjoyed it, as a small publisher we rely on word of mouth so please recommend it to others.